Twayne's English Authors Series

Sylvia E. Bowman, *Editor*

INDIANA UNIVERSITY

Sydney Smith

 50

Sydney Smith

By SHELDON HALPERN

Bowling Green State University

Twayne Publishers, Inc.　::　New York

To my Ems

Preface

The best known wit of his own generation and the most widely quoted of the next, Sydney Smith has suffered a severe decline in reputation during the twentieth century. In England, biographies and collections of his writings have appeared with some regularity; but in the United States, he is virtually unknown, even among students of literature. His essays are included in none of the text anthologies, and the only American collection of his writings to appear this century was edited by W. H. Auden, a transplanted Briton.

Smith is, to be sure, a minor writer, but not so minor that he should be allowed to slip into oblivion. Aside from the sheer fun that his essays and pamphlets still hold for the modern reader, Smith has a great deal to say on a number of topics that are as current today as they were a century and a half ago—toleration, the relationship between church and state, the purposes of education, and the equality of justice. A profound knowledge of early nineteenth-century England is not essential to an appreciation of his wit or point; for, though he characteristically addressed himself to particular issues, he always included enough significant background to keep a reader informed. And the human follies and foibles which his wit satirized are those of all men, found in but not restricted to his particular victims.

Hopefully, a general survey such as this study can serve to reintroduce Smith to the American reader. For this reason, I have tried to discuss the complete range of Smith's writings, from sermons to letters. He was a master of a wide variety of styles, all of which are illustrated and discussed in these pages. But my major emphasis has not been belletristic criticism for the very good reason that Smith was a public more than a literary man. His work involves issues, not themes; arguments, not architectonics. Therefore, my main task has been to discuss his ideas and opinions within the context of his life and times, and, I hope, with relevance to our own.

Because he was so public a man, most biographies of Smith

place great emphasis on his jokes, anecdotes, conversation, and personal correspondence. This practice is as it should be, for Smith did not reserve all his good things for the press; he was a brilliant conversationalist at all times. Yet I have kept such material to a minimum, preferring, within the limits of a short book, to discuss his published writings as fully as possible, the only appropriate attitude for one of a series of volumes on English authors.

As the first American to write a book-length study of Smith, I have felt a particular obligation to rectify the false view of his attitudes toward the United States, a view which has contributed greatly to his general neglect in this country. I have, therefore, devoted an entire chapter, the sixth, to this issue, in hopes of removing a major obstacle to wider recognition in America of the particular genius of Sydney Smith.

This book began as a doctoral dissertation in the Faculty of Philosophy of Columbia University. I am grateful and indebted for comments and suggestions to Professors Charles Everett, John H. Middendorf, Marshall Suther, Robert K. Webb, and Carl R. Woodring, who read it in that form, and especially to Professor Lionel Trilling, who directed my research and writing from the beginning. Thanks are also due to my former colleagues in South Bend, John A. Cassidy and Francis J. Molson, who, to their bad luck and my good fortune, occupied offices adjoining mine and bore up patiently under constant requests for reading, comment, and reaction. For their aid to my research, I must express my gratitude to the Newberry Library and the libraries of Columbia, Indiana, Notre Dame, and Bowling Green State universities; to William G. Lane and Esther Rhoads Houghton, who put me on to valuable material; and to David Holland, who placed at my disposal copies of the unpublished memoirs of Catherine Amelia Smith. Sylvia E. Bowman's editorial guidance has been invaluable. Most of all, I thank my typist, first editor, copyreader, proofreader—and wife, Marilyn Halpern. Thanks are due to The Clarendon Press, Oxford, for permission to quote from *The Letters of Sydney Smith*, edited by Nowell C. Smith.

S. H.

Bowling Green State University
Bowling Green, Ohio

Contents

Chronology

bendary of Bristol Cathedral. Stops writing for *Edinburgh Review.*

1829   Death of Douglas Smith. Exchanges living of Foston for Combe Florey, Somersetshire.

1831   Appointed Canon Residentiary of St. Paul's Cathedral.

1834   Saba Smith marries Dr. Henry Holland.

1837– *Letters to Archdeacon Singleton* published in three pam-
1839   phlets.

1839   *Ballot,* a pamphlet, and *Works,* in three volumes, published.

1843   *Letters on American Debts* published.

1845   Dies in London, February 22.

CHAPTER 1

Coming Up Stairs

I *Second Son*

IN THE midst of his career, when Sydney Smith had become a widely read essayist and an established parochial clergyman, he had a motto painted on his carriage: *Faber meae fortunae*— the smith of my own fortune. Born into the middle class, Smith had risen to a position of great influence in letters, in the church, and in the highest circles of society and politics through his own efforts and abilities, aided neither by fortune nor by family.

His grandfather had moved from Devon to Eastcheap early in the eighteenth century and prospered as a dealer in Witney cloth, a heavy woolen. Robert Smith, Sydney's father, was the oldest of two brothers and three sisters. Born in 1738 or 1739 and orphaned while still a young man, Robert Smith had little zeal for the family business he had inherited; and, as soon as his younger brother John was old enough to take over, Robert sold out to him for a sum sufficient to insure a small income and went to seek his fortune in America.

Upon his return to England, Robert Smith proposed marriage to Maria Olier, the daughter of a French Huguenot merchant who had left Languedoc upon the revocation of the Edict of Nantes. He asked Maria's widowed mother to allow him to return to America in order to attend to some business he had started there and to marry Maria on his return, in about two years. Mrs. Olier, who would not bind her daughter to so distant an event, agreed only to reconsider his suit when he came back, if neither his feelings nor Maria's had changed in the meantime. Unwilling to take a chance of losing either his bride or his American investments, Robert Smith pretended to forego his intended journey; married Miss Olier at St. George's Church, Bloomsbury; and, leaving his new wife at the church door, set out for America. He returned after a few years of useless wandering and settled down as much as his restless nature would allow. In the course of his married life, he engaged in ruinous speculation in real estate, buying, altering, and selling (usually at a loss) about nineteen different properties. In addition to this constant movement about the English countryside, he was frequently away on trips to Spain, France, or Italy, leaving his wife at home to care for her growing family.

What he lacked in responsibility he made up for in personal charm. He had a natural eloquence, an extraordinarily retentive memory for anecdotes and social gossip, and a striking appearance which he emphasized by wearing the drab-colored dress of a Quaker. The wife whom he had attracted by such unsubstantial qualities was a far better mother than he was a father. His long absences from home and the family's frequent changes of residence added to the normal difficulties of rearing five children. Robert Percy was born in 1770; Sydney, in 1771; Cecil, in 1772; Courtenay, in 1773; and Maria, in 1774. Their mother's warm but naturally nervous temperament was overstrained by the physical and emotional difficulties of life with Robert Smith, and she was subject to attacks of a nervous disease from which she died in 1802, twenty-five years before the death of her husband.

Although the Smith children probably inherited their intelligence and quick minds from their father, there was enough of their mother in them to turn their high spirits and keen minds to more useful occupations than globe-trotting and losing money. The four boys were all good scholars at an early age. Their mother directed their studies and took pride in their accomplishments. They used to read books supposedly beyond their years, and discussed their readings with the kind of enthusiasm and competition most children devote to games.

Sydney was sent at the age of six to a school in Southampton kept by the Reverend Mr. Marsh. In 1782, all four boys were sent to public schools, their expenses paid by the schools' foundations. Robert Percy and Cecil went to Eton, Sydney and Courtenay to Winchester, the two elder boys each being expected to keep a watchful eye on his younger brother. Conditions at the public schools at the time were deplorable; the boys were subjected, by the fagging system, to the tyranny and cruelty of those in upper forms. Food was meager and often uneatable. The studies themselves were almost exclusively Latin and Greek grammar and verse-making.

Though Sydney did exceptionally well as a student, he could never look back with calmness or pleasure on his school days. Many years later, in the *Edinburgh Review,* he attacked public schools, saying, "In by far the greatest number of cases, we cannot think public schools favourable to the cultivation of knowledge; and we have equally strong doubts if they be so to the cultivation of morals." [1] Even later, as Canon of St. Paul's, when he found himself in charge of the care and education of the choirboys, his own unhappy experience at Winchester guided him in making sure that his young charges were well fed, well housed, well clothed, and well taught.

In addition to his own hardships at school, Sydney had the problem of caring for Courtenay, who was so discouraged by the harshness of school life that he twice ran away. But the studious habits and self-assurance which had been bred into the boys by their mother overcame the depressing conditions under which they lived, and they both earned academic distinctions. Courtenay won the gold medal for Latin verse for four consecutive years until his schoolmates successfully petitioned the headmaster to exclude him from competition. And Sydney became, in his last year at Winchester, Prefect of the Hall, the title given the head boy of the school.

Robert Percy and Cecil were encountering similarly mixed experiences at Eton. The eldest Smith acquired the nickname of Bobus at school and kept it all his life. He had a greater reputation for literary ability in school and college than Sydney; and with George Canning, John Hookham Frere, and a boy named John Smith, he started a weekly paper at Eton called the *Microcosm* which, under the nom de plume of Gregory Griffin, made the boys known beyond the halls of the school. Bobus went on to King's College, Cambridge, where he was noted for the beauty of his Latin verses. Later called to the bar, Bobus acquired a wide reputation for honesty and learning.

Both Cecil and Courtenay were sent to India immediately after public school through the influence of a Mr. Roberts, Chairman of the East India Company and an old friend of Robert Smith. Of the four boys, Cecil most resembled their father in habits. As a youth he was more extravagant and careless than his brothers, and as a man he was the most improvident. Starting as a clerk, he rose to be Accountant-General in Madras, but his large salary never sufficed for his expenses. He seems also to have had some marital difficulties; and he was in conflict with his superiors more than once. In 1807 Cecil was accused of irregularities in his accounts, and in 1809 he was involved in a military mutiny against the Governor of Madras. In both instances he was cleared of charges and reinstated, largely through his brothers' influence in London. He was on his way home on a leave of absence in 1814 when he died, almost penniless, at the Cape of Good Hope.

Courtenay Smith started in a similar clerkship in Calcutta. He became Supreme Judge over a vast area of India and a noted Oriental scholar. He returned to England in 1825 and remained a bachelor all his life, living simply. Although Courtenay had no quarrel with Sydney or Bobus, he kept to himself after his retirement and did not seem at all eager to renew family ties. He died intestate in 1843, and the great wealth he had amassed in the East was divided among his two living brothers and Cecil's orphaned son.

Sydney's achievements at Winchester and performance on an examination entitled him to a scholarship at New College, Oxford. He was admitted on the occurrence of a vacancy in February, 1789; but before taking up residence at the University, he was sent by his father to live for six months in France. It was by no means the Grand Tour, but it was an opportunity to learn French and to live abroad for a time. It was also almost the only expense his father ever went to for the sake of Sydney's education. When he entered Oxford as a scholar, he was provided by his college with room, food, and tuition. He must have had some allowance from his father (Bobus at Cambridge was given two hundred and fifty pounds a year), but it must have been a small one; for, when in 1791 Sydney received a fellowship of one hundred pounds a year, he stopped drawing on his father altogether. He held this fellowship until his marriage in 1800, and for his three remaining years at Oxford it was his only income. Without the means of providing the kind of vinous hospitality common in New College at the time, Sydney chose solitude rather than accepting invitations he could not afford to return without going into debt.

Sydney wanted to follow Bobus into the law, a profession for which he felt eminently suited, but his father refused this request. Having undertaken to educate his first son for the bar, Robert Smith could not or would not bear the expense of doing as much for his second. He appealed once more to his friend Mr. Roberts in an attempt to ship Sydney out to the Orient and was promised an appointment for the young man as supercargo of an East Indiaman bound for Macao. But at the last moment the post was given to someone else, saving Sydney from the seemingly inevitable expatriation of the Smiths. (Bobus later spent eight years in India.) "You may be a college tutor or a parson," Sydney was told by his father. Five wretched years at Oxford had not endeared the academic life to him, and so, more in resignation to his father's whims than in obedience to his father's wishes, Sydney sought a career in the Church of England.

Six years later, when he married, Sydney Smith once more came into violent conflict with his father over money matters. On July 2, 1800, he married Catherine Amelia Pybus, of Cheam, the daughter of a deceased Bond Street banker. Catherine Pybus had known the Smith family for a long time, having been a schoolmate of Maria. The wedding took place at Cheam, over the objections of the bride's brother Charles, a self-important petty office-holder in the Pitt government, who did not care for Smith's poverty or opposition politics. But the young couple had the blessings of Mrs. Pybus, who had known and admired Sydney Smith for some time and had approved their engagement two years before.

Smith described his fiancée in a letter written ten months before his marriage. "She is 3 years younger than me, a very old friend of mine—a good figure—& to *me* an interesting countenance —of excellent disposition, extremely good Sense, very fond of music, & me—a wise amiable woman such as without imposing specious qualities will quietly for years & years make the happiness of her husband's Life." [2] Smith insisted that his wife's entire personal fortune, as well as any future money that should be left her, be placed in trust for her exclusive use, so that he should not be able to touch it; and it was only after Catherine and her mother both argued that some provision must be made for emergencies that he allowed them to place one thousand pounds at his disposal. He wanted the money beyond his reach not only to show that he did not want his wife's wealth, but also to forestall his father from making any demands on him for capital with which to buy land. At first, Catherine thought this an exaggerated caution, but when she and her bridegroom visited his family, she was amazed to hear her father-in-law abuse his son for the action. "You *knew* I wished to purchase a farm," Robert Smith said, "your *Father* should have been first thought of! What right had *you*, where you had it in your power to benefit *me*, to indulge in such silly romantic notions of securing to her her property? Could it be anywhere safer than in the hands of your *Father?*" [3]

The older Smith's proven incompetence in money matters was reason enough to keep Catherine's small fortune out of his hands. In addition, there was no reason for Sydney to feel any obligation or gratitude toward his father. His Oxford fellowship had relieved his father of his university expenses; but when he had asked for some allowance upon his marriage, by which he lost the fellowship, he met with a flat refusal. The hard feelings between father and son which were caused by this financial squabbling lasted for over four years, and other effects lasted much longer. The scenes of his honeymoon visit to his family left Sydney Smith with a horrible warning of the dangers of marriage on insecure and insufficient income. He was subject to fits of depression for many years before his gradually improving financial situation and happy family life convinced him that he would not be the failure his father had been. But the experience of his early manhood had left him with a sensitivity to insult and a need for independence which ill became a clergyman and literary man dependent on the wealthy and powerful for his career.

During the summer of 1800, while Smith was brooding upon his own and his wife's financial insecurity, he was invited to come, with his bride, on a tour of England, as guests of Mr. and Mrs. Michael Hicks Beach. The Beaches were Smith's patrons, in that they had employed him as a tutor to their sons; but their gracious behavior to him was repaid in an unusual way. Soon after the tour, Smith wrote to Mrs. Beach, accusing her of slighting Mrs. Smith during the tour and of treating her in a proud and contemptuous manner. After an exchange of letters, Smith's apparent wrath cooled, and he remained the Beaches' tutor for three more years.[4]

The whole ridiculous altercation probably resulted from Smith's new awareness of the responsibilities of marriage and from his reaction to his father's selfish conduct. The combination of resentment of his own poverty and guilt for bringing a wife to share it threw Smith into a mood of depression in which he lashed out at the handiest object. In this case it was Mrs. Beach, who not only represented the kind of wealth and station he could not give Catherine, but whose continued employment of him was the financial crutch which made him recognize his own inability to make his way, unaided, in the world.

The pride and independence which prompted him to attack and take offense at his superiors rather than to flatter or patronize them never left him. But the kind of wrathful moralization which had been heaped on Mrs. Beach found a more useful outlet in his essays, which pointed out the unjust, deflated the pompous, and flogged the greedy with effective, and often cruel, wit.

II *The Parallelogram*

Sydney Smith's rise from the penniless obscurity of his early days as an unbeneficed clergyman was an achievement due mostly to his own ability, but made possible by fortunate circumstances. One was the marriage of Bobus Smith to Miss Caroline Vernon, the daughter of Evelyn, first Countess of Upper Ossory, by her second husband, Richard Vernon. Caroline Vernon Smith's two elder half sisters, Ladies Mary and Louisa Fitzpatrick, the daughters of Lord Upper Ossory, had married William Petty, first Marquess of Lansdowne (better known as the Earl of Shelburne), and Stephen Fox, second Baron Holland, respectively. When Sydney Smith performed his brother's marriage ceremony at Bowood, the Lansdowne estate, on December 9, 1797, he formed a connection between his family and the landed aristocracy that was to serve as his introduction to the highest circles of English society.

He became acquainted with two young men, nephews of Bobus' wife and future leaders of Whig society and politics, who were to be his lifelong friends. One was Lord Henry Petty, later third

Marquess of Lansdowne. The other, whose friendship with Smith was closer and whose influence was more important in establishing Smith's future career, was Richard Henry Fox, third Baron Holland. His grandfather, Henry Fox, using his talents and political connections as Paymaster of the Treasury, had built up an estate by laying out public money for his own interest. Thirty years after he took the office, his heirs were still paying back what was owed to the nation—but a family fortune had been made and a peerage acquired. Young Lord Holland's uncle, Charles James Fox, was the acknowledged leader of the aristocratic and liberal interest in Parliament until his death in 1806. Though Holland's eloquence was not able to inspire the kind of fervid devotion that had been given to Fox, his warm and frank disposition, personal charm, and private virtues gave him great influence in society and in the House of Lords.

Lady Holland had been born Elizabeth Vassal, the daughter of a wealthy Jamaica planter. Married at sixteen to the middle-aged Sir Godfrey Webster, and discontented with life at her dull husband's dull Sussex estate, she insisted on traveling abroad. She first met Lord Holland in Italy in 1795, when she was twenty-five and he twenty-one. They eloped, had a son in 1796, and were married in 1797 after her divorce from Sir Godfrey. Lady Holland was never accepted by most of the women of the aristocracy, but her beauty, intelligence, wit, and vivacity soon attracted to Holland House some of the most able and noted men of the day. Her selfishness, bad temper, and imperious manner amused rather than offended her wide circle of devoted friends, and Holland House became a center for all that was brilliant and sophisticated among the Whig aristocrats of the early nineteenth century.

The Whig aristocracy itself, the brilliant, eccentric, snobbish, fantastically wealthy society into which Holland House launched Sydney Smith, was an astounding phenomenon. Smith said, in later years, "I believe the parallelogram between Oxford Street, Piccadilly, Regent Street, and Hyde Park, incloses more intelligence and human ability, to say nothing of wealth and beauty, than the world has ever collected in such a space before." [5] The aristocrats who inhabited the fashionable West End of London certainly earned this description, and more.

Their immense wealth, almost entirely in land, brought them

annual incomes running into five, and sometimes six, figures. Expensive vices like gambling, drinking, and adultery, and expensive tastes like traveling, collecting art, and building estates seemed unable to make irreparable inroads into their rent-rolls; and the smooth life of the aristocrats went on through all eventualities and all seasons. They spent the warmer half of the year on their country estates, hunting, shooting, looking to the harvests and the rents, visiting, and receiving guests. Ladies made visits of charity to the village poor; and gentlemen, acting as Justices of the Peace, sat in judgment on village poachers. Most of all, they cultivated their "influence"—that combination of bribery, coercion, and respect which insured them of the political loyalty of tenants and tradesmen and gave them the right to nominate members of Parliament.

Throughout the "season," the six months of the year during which the English aristocracy gathered in the magic parallelogram of Mayfair, there was constant social activity. Every meal was an opportunity for hospitality and conversation. Late-morning breakfasts left the afternoon for strolls, visits, rides through the park, and teas. Dinner, served some time between eight and ten o'clock, was midday for society and a high point in the daily routine. Seven courses and a variety of wines were consumed while diamonds and talk sparkled among the well-dressed company. After dinner there were plays, balls, routs, or sessions at card tables. Midnight suppers were light affairs, and the small quantity of food was balanced by a great quantity of wine and spirits.

But the main purpose keeping the aristocracy in London during the "season" was Parliament. If some particularly controversial measure were under discussion, gentlemen of the aristocracy forsook amusement for the serious business of debate until dawn. For under all the social activity, the English aristocracy was a political body. After the Whig nobles had established William and Mary in the Glorious Revolution, excluded the Roman Catholic Duke of York in the later seventeenth century, and finally brought about the Hanoverian succession with its limited monarchy, they became the dominant force in politics. With a great voice in a small House of Lords (there were only 174 British peers at the accession of George III in 1760) and with well-established influence in the House of Commons, they controlled Parliament. Under George I and George II, especially during the long term of Sir Robert Walpole, the old Tory opposition dwindled away to a small number of die-hard Jacobites and some members of the country squirearchy who still felt a feudal loyalty to the Crown.

In becoming the ruling class, the landed aristocrats ceased to be a political party. They all called themselves Whigs, and their central principles became lost in the factionalism which made up political activity during most of the eighteenth century. Statesmen went into cabinet office, not because they declared a policy acceptable to the King and to a majority of Parliament, but because they were able to call upon sufficient influence to insure their success in running the affairs of government. A skillful politician, like the Duke of Newcastle or the Earl of Chatham, could count on gathering a number of followers with enough votes in each House to support his measures. Nobles gave their influence in return for patronage—peerages or cabinet posts for themselves; promotions in the church, army, or navy, or seats in the House of Commons for their younger sons; government places and sinecures for other relatives and dependents. Every seven years, or oftener in case of a dissolution, a general election would take place, with borough patrons demanding promises of future patronage from ministers before seating some government candidate as a duly elected representative, and factions spending huge sums to bribe electorates which could not be completely mastered by aristocratic influence. If the election managers failed to bring in the predicted results or the promised patronage did not materialize, new alignments were made, new promises were elicited, and a new government might emerge to try its luck. All called themselves "Whigs" and identified their opposition of the hour as "Tories," but the real political contest was among groups of followers of professional statesmen, whose commitment was to keeping themselves in office and their dependents in places.

George III, determined to attach more direct power to the throne than his grandfather or great-grandfather had achieved or even aspired to, began to bring into the government men like Lord Bute, committed to the King rather than to the aristocracy. Some were old Jacobites and genuine Tories, some were placeholders in the bureaucracy. By the late eighteenth century, the court party had great strength among the clergy of the Church of England, the petty gentry of the squirearchy, and the professional civil servants who saw their best chance of survival in adherence to the Crown rather than to any political faction. In 1780, the Whig aristocracy, rebelling against the King's insistence that he dictate policy to his ministers (in this case, nonrecognition of American independence and pursuit of the war), passed the famous resolution, "That the influence of the Crown has increased, is increasing, and ought to be diminished." But it was too late for the aristocracy to unite against the King. The American Revolution brought more nobles over to the side of the court, and then the French Revolution brought fear of any anti-monarchial sentiments and firmly established a pro-Church-and-King majority that controlled the affairs of Britain for over thirty years with only one brief Whig interlude.

By the time of the younger Pitt's death in 1806, the court party was in reality a political party, universally recognized as Tory, and dedicated to support of the King against the Parliament and maintenance of the privileged establishment of the Church of England by any means necessary. In opposition, the Whigs rallied around the causes of religious toleration and, later, Parliamentary reform as means to diminish the power of the Crown and its chief adherents. They strengthened their ranks in Commons by bringing in young men of talent and liberal principles for the many boroughs whose nominations they controlled. They welcomed able men of the middle class, like Samuel Romilly and Samuel Whitbread, who had become wealthy enough in trades or professions to buy their way into Parliament and support Whig causes.

But political ties with the middle class did not imply any notions of social equality on the part of the aristocracy. Gentlemen of the ruling class who sat on opposite sides of the House during violent debate could face each other with equanimity and even real affection across a dinner table; but no tradesman, whatever his principles, politics, or even wealth, expected to be received into their company. Certain professions—the church, the bar, the armed services, and, of course, the House of Commons—afforded avenues by which the middle class might send its children into polite society, but other professions and all businesses had the taint of "trade" that excluded those who practiced them from the drawing rooms of the great.

The same conviction of their own irrefutable superiority that prompted the aristocrats' snobbery and exclusion of all outsiders allowed them to patronize individuals of lower classes whose exceptional talents of one sort or another made them worth displaying. An eloquent talker like Richard Brinsley Sheridan or an arbiter of taste and fashion like Beau Brummell could be taken up by the powerful and made to feel, for a while, like one of the charmed circle. But the protégé was expected to know his place, to realize that he had been elevated by special permission and not by right. Samuel Rogers said, "Society is so constituted in England, that it is useless for celebrated artists to think of bringing their families into the highest circles, where themselves are admitted only on account of their genius. Their wives and daughters must be content to remain at home." [6] Rogers had his great wealth as a banker to protect him from the vicissitudes of noble patronage, but both Sheridan and Brummell ended their careers in wretched poverty, once they had lost the favor of their noble friends.

If Brummell's career as a protégé of the Whig aristocracy was the most brilliant of the age, Sydney Smith's was among the most stable. Other figures appear only briefly in the annals of social England, but almost every memoir, diary, or collection of correspondence from the first half of the nineteenth century contains descriptions of Smith's humor or quotations of his wit. And in the letters, journals, and even poetic effusions of his wide circle of friends, he is referred to as "Sydney" more frequently than as "Smith"—at a time when the use of Christian names was far from common.

Smith is perhaps best known from the period during which he was a Canon of St. Paul's and resident in London for half the year, an intimate of the upper classes, a much-sought-after dinner guest, and a conversationalist who had entree wherever talent was admired. He must have appeared at that time very like the caricature which Thackeray did of him, dressed in the knee breeches and stockings of the previous generation with four buttons of his well-filled waistcoat protruding from beneath a deep-collared cutaway coat. His profile, though far from handsome, is arresting; and his large hooked nose, strong chin, dark eyebrows, and high forehead surmounted by a crest of white hair keep his round face from being bland.

However, long before his appointment to high church office, Smith was introduced to Whig society through Holland House and earned a place in the magic parallelogram of wit and wealth, brilliance and beauty that he saw as the crowning social glory of English culture. Richard Monckton Milnes, Lord Houghton, recorded of Smith, "I remember his vision of an immense Square with the trees flowering with flambeaux, with gas for grass, and every window illuminated by countless chandeliers, and voices reiterating for ever and for ever, 'Mr. Sydney Smith coming up stairs!' " [7]

III *Tenui Musam Meditamur Avena*

If his acquaintance with Lord Holland gave Sydney Smith the opportunity to enter aristocratic society, his renown as one of the young men who had started a new kind of critical journal gave him the reputation for literary talent that made his entrance feasible. Smith's account of the founding of the *Edinburgh Review* in 1802 is found in the preface to his collected works.

The principles of the French Revolution were then fully afloat, and it is impossible to conceive a more violent and agitated state of society. Among the first persons with whom I became acquainted [in Edinburgh] were, Lord Jeffrey, Lord Murray (late Lord Advocate for Scotland), and Lord Brougham, all of them maintaining opinions upon political subjects a little too liberal for the dynasty of Dundas, then exercising supreme power over the northern division of the island.

One day we happened to meet in the eighth or ninth story or flat in Buccleugh-place, the elevated residence of the then Mr. Jeffrey. I proposed that we should set up a Review; this was acceded to with acclamation. I was appointed Editor, and remained long enough in Edinburgh to edit the first number of the Edinburgh Review. The motto I proposed for the Review was,
> *"Tenui musam meditamur avena"*
> "We cultivate literature upon a little oatmeal." [8]

The beginnings of the *Edinburgh Review* were neither so simple nor so harmonious as this description implies, but in substance the account is accurate.[9] There must have been a number of meetings among Smith, Henry Brougham, Francis Jeffrey, and John A. Murray, as well as other associates in the venture, Francis Horner, Thomas Brown, Thomas Thomson, and John Thomson. Such eminent Edinburgh intellectuals as Walter Scott and professors Dugald Stewart and John Playfair contributed a few articles. Brougham points out in his memoirs that Smith was "quasi-editor" for the first number, in that he collected various articles and saw the review through the press, but that Smith lacked the scientific and mathematical knowledge and strong classical erudition necessary for a regular editorship.[10]

As a matter of fact, Brougham himself was among the last of the circle to commit himself to the review. He was not sure that he wanted to risk his legal career by being associated with the socially unacceptable profession of writing for the periodical press. A number of years later, even after he was well-known as a reviewer, he was sensitive about having the fact mentioned publicly. On one occasion he bought a book at the shop which served as the London agency for the *Edinburgh Review* and was infuriated when a clerk shouted from the back, "Was it to be charged to Mr. B's private account or to the *Edinburgh Review*." [11] Brougham did not withdraw his reservations until Jeffrey officially became editor and Smith confined his attentions to his own articles.

Brougham was not the only one among the reviewers who was pleased to see Jeffrey replace Smith as editor. Although Smith did not have, or try to exercise, the kind of authority that later became Jeffrey's, he did a certain amount of revision of the work of others for the first few numbers; and he was certainly responsible for the final form of his own work, even though he frequently sought Jeffrey's advice on matters of style and taste. Smith so revised Thomas Brown's review of Mme de Sousa's *Charles et Marie* in the third number that Brown publicly withdrew from the journal, and Smith put a notice in the *Edinburgh* that the Editor was solely responsible for certain alterations in the article.[12] Smith's own writings were singled out for specific mention in several attacks on the generally caustic tone of the *Edinburgh Review*. Isaac D'Israeli, in a burlesque upon the founding of the journal, describes a scene in which, "One of their great critics, a ludicrous genius of a parson, started up, with his cassock in tatters, and flinging his pantaloon cap in the air, he exclaimed—'Without a squeeze of lemon, how the devil could the constable expect to make the REVIEW sell!' " [13] Sir Alexander Boswell, in a poem praising the *Edinburgh Review*, takes exception to Smith's witty but unworthy attacks on Dr. Parr and Dr. Langford in the first number.[14]

Francis Horner, a staunch friend and fellow reviewer, wrote to a friend that the first number contained "certain articles, which most of us, before they were printed, considered as exceptionable on that very account [of tone and manner.]" That some of the articles Horner referred to were Smith's seems evident from a subsequent letter to the same friend, in which Horner announces the appearance of the second number and states, "I think you will find it free, at least nearly so, from some of the objections that were most strongly, and all of them justly, urged against the former. There are scarcely any insignificant books,—no sermons—few personalities—the general train of criticism less abusive." [15] The allusions to sermons and personalities are particularly applicable to Smith's contributions to the first number, notably his reviews of books and sermons by Parr, Rennel, Langford, Nares, and Bowles.

Though Smith's work as editor of his own and others' writing may have been found somewhat wanting in the early days of the review, his work as manager of the enterprise was not. First and foremost, his was the original suggestion for the journal, and it was his encouragement and insistence that kept the brilliant circle of young men together long enough to get the review established. His grasp of practical necessities led to a financial arrangement that allowed the *Edinburgh Review* to set a new, independent tone in periodical criticism. Early in 1803, Archibald Constable, an Edinburgh bookseller and publisher, asked Smith his opinion of the probable success of the *Edinburgh Review*.

Smith replied that its continuation seemed inevitable. "It is notorious that all the reviews are the organs either of party or of booksellers. I have no manner of doubt that an *able, intrepid,* and *independent* review would be as useful to the public as it would be profitable to those who are engaged in it." [16] Smith entered into negotiations with Constable and T. N. Longman and convinced them that they should give fifty pounds a number, or two hundred pounds a year, to an editor, and ten guineas a sheet (sixteen pages in the octavo review) to contributors. Jeffrey, who was to be the editor, wrote to Horner to tell him of the arrangements. "The terms are, as Mr. Longman says, 'without precedent;' . . . All the men here will take their ten guineas, I find, and . . . I think I may take my editor's salary also without being supposed to have suffered any degradation."

The insistence of the review upon paying all its contributors relieved each of the social stigma of journalism; so long as payment was uniform none could be accused of writing merely for money, and Jeffrey was able to inform his brother two months later, with greater confidence, "The publication is in the highest degree respectable as yet, as there are none but gentlemen connected with it. If it ever sinks into the state of an ordinary bookseller's journal, I have done with it." [17] The Edinburgh Review never did, in Jeffrey's opinion, sink to the state of an ordinary bookseller's journal; for he stayed on as editor for over a quarter of a century, becoming the most influential, if not necessarily the most astute, critic of his time. He always considered the law his real career, however, and willingly left the review in 1829 when he was appointed to the bench.

The principle that all those engaged in writing and editing the Edinburgh Review were gentlemen, paid for their contributions and services but still amateur men of letters, was mainly responsible for the journal's success. The absence of the taint of trade attracted men of the upper-middle class and even of the nobility, men with university educations and independent of the whims and wishes of publishers, to write articles for the review. Brougham claimed that, "The first effect of our Review, absolutely independent of the trade and of any party in the country, local or general, was to raise the character and increase the influence of periodical criticism." The Edinburgh offered a welcome relief to the discriminating reader from a large number of contemporary reviews written by Grub Street hacks and published by booksellers in order to promote their own works or attack those of competitors.[18] Starting in 1802 with a circulation of eight hundred, the review had nine thousand subscribers by 1808 when Walter Scott said that "no genteel family can pretend to be without it, because . . . it gives the only valuable literary criticism which can be met with." [19] The following year, Scott and others who objected to the *Edinburgh's* politics founded the *Quarterly Review*. Both journals reached their peak circulations of about fourteen thousand each, in 1818; in addition, the *Edinburgh* was sold in book form, two numbers to a volume.

The form of the *Edinburgh Review*, imitated by the *Quarterly*, set the pattern for critical periodicals to this day. Articles were by men of wide learning, who often used the books under discussion as points of departure for penetrating essays on subjects which only remotely resembled those of the works being reviewed. Thus the review served as a source not only of criticism but also of social commentary, political and religious polemic, new ideas in the sciences and the infant social sciences, and general information.

Just as important as the *Edinburgh Review's* independence from booksellers was its independence from political parties. Periodical writers and publications at that time were heavily controlled by political interests, through direct government subsidies, placement of official advertising, or financial takeovers during election campaigns. Though the general political tone of the *Edinburgh Review* reflected the opinions of C. J. Fox and his followers, it never became an official organ of the Whig party, and it attacked abuses and praised worth-while causes wherever it found them. Lord Cockburn, in his biography of Jeffrey, credits the *Edinburgh Review* with helping to bring about reforms in such areas as religious toleration; the slave trade; popular education; the condition of Ireland; military justice; the treatment of the insane, the criminal, and the insolvent; the status of the physical sciences; and the general attitude toward reforming antiquated and unjust institutions. Smith and Brougham made similar lists.[20]

While the intelligence and independence of the *Edinburgh Review* made it enlightening and exciting, the brilliant wit and humor of Smith was a major factor in making it amusing and readable. In his articles, readers found the same social and political liberalism that characterized Jeffrey, Horner, and Brougham presented in a light yet penetrating way that made them eager to welcome him as a man of talent to their dinner tables and salons.

CHAPTER 2

Practical Religion

I   *Place-hunting*

THE situation of Sydney Smith, entering the clergy of the
Church of England as one would enter any of the learned
professions in order to make an honest and respectable living, was
not an unusual one at that time. The church offered a potentially
lucrative career to a young man with talent and good connections,
and the close relationship between the power of the laity and the
authority of the church made clerical advancement a matter of
social and political influence. Almost all church livings were paid
from the rents on land, and many of the appointments were made
directly by lay proprietors: landowners, noblemen, or members
of the government. Other livings were part of the patronage of
cathedrals or episcopal sees. Few, if any, appointments were made
according to the wishes of the congregation or strictly on the
basis of pastoral abilities. Political belief was often a criterion for
promotion, and Archbishop Markham of York warned his clergy
in 1781 that for them to join parliamentary reform associations
would be "foreign to their clerical functions, and not the road to
preferment." [1]

Unbeneficed clergymen had to do the best they could by
preaching in private chapels, serving noblemen or institutions
as chaplains, or substituting for nonresident vicars as curates,
while they sought the patronage of those influential enough to
get them secure places in the ecclesiastical structure. Income var-
ied widely among the lower clergy, and many livings were too
small to be the sole support of a family man. In 1810, there were
3,998 livings of one hundred and fifty pounds a year or less in England and Wales, and fewer than one-third of these were over one
hundred pounds.[2] Living on such a pittance after the expense of
a university education, the least materialistic men waited in con-

stant hope for promotion as clergymen in order to be able to live like gentlemen.

Yet for the fortunate few who rose to become canons, deans, or bishops, or even for the larger number who received some of the rich livings, the church could lead to significant material success. Sydney Smith never pretended to be in a profession that precluded all thought of self, and so long as he was not required to go against his personal, religious, or political convictions, he saw nothing wrong in seeking preferment. Without any private fortune or income to support his family, he felt duty bound to press for his due when someone on whom he had a claim could benefit his career.

Smith's first patron was Mr. Michael Hicks Beach, M. P. for Cirencester and landowner of the village of Netheravon near Amesbury, Wiltshire. How Smith first made his acquaintance is not known, but during the summer of 1794, at the request of Hicks Beach, the absentee vicar of Netheravon appointed as his curate, at fifty pounds a year, the newly ordained Deacon Mr. Sydney Smith. The solitude and bleakness of this Salisbury Plain hamlet was not worth the small measure of professional security the post offered, and by the spring of 1796 Smith was seeking his future elsewhere. In 1797, he was again offered a post by Hicks Beach, this time as tutor to the squire's son, with whom Smith took up residence in Edinburgh in June, 1798.

In Edinburgh, and later in London, Smith found professional employment as a chapel preacher. In the Scottish capital, he preached a number of sermons in Charlotte Chapel, six of which he published in 1800 as his first work. In London, the friendship of Sir Thomas Bernard, an active philanthropist, resulted in Smith's being appointed evening preacher at the Foundling Hospital. He was also appointed morning preacher at two private chapels, Berkeley Chapel and Fitzroy Chapel, where he delivered sermons on alternate Sunday mornings from 1804 to 1809.

Such preacherships were professional employment, but were neither secure nor substantial. It took a change of political fortunes for real advancement to come to Sydney Smith. A number of his Whig friends joined the coalition "Ministry of All the Talents" that was formed in January, 1806, and collapsed in March,

1807. Lord Holland procured for Smith from Lord Chancellor Erskine an appointment as Rector of Foston, a parish in a remote section of Yorkshire. For a while, Smith was able to remain in London and receive the five hundred pounds' annual income from Foston, pleading his Foundling Hospital duties as an excuse for not living on his Yorkshire parish. In 1809, however, a new Archbishop of York invoked the Clergy Residence Act against him, and he had to move to the north. His new parish did not even have a habitable rectory, and after four years of fruitless attempts to get a better situation, Smith went deeply into debt to build a home for his family. In 1823, his situation improved a little when Lady Georgiana Morpeth, the daughter-in-law of Smith's Yorkshire neighbor, Lord Carlisle, asked her brother, the Duke of Devonshire, to present Smith with the living of Londesborough, worth eight hundred pounds a year. Smith held this living as a plurality until 1832, when Lady Morpeth's son, William George Howard, for whom the living was eventually intended, came of age and entered holy orders.

In 1827, a coalition government formed under George Canning brought Whigs into the cabinet for the first time since 1807. This change in the political climate brought Smith clerical fruits. In January, 1828, he was appointed to a prebendary stall at Bristol Cathedral. His living of Foston was exchanged for that of Combe Florey, near Taunton, Somersetshire; and the Dean and Chapter of Bristol Cathedral presented him with the small additional living of Halberton. Smith's success in achieving both financial security and a situation near London was crowned in September, 1831, when Lord Grey, Prime Minister of a new, reform-minded Whig government, appointed him Canon Residentiary of St. Paul's Cathedral. In every instance, Smith's promotion within the church had been brought about by the influence of friendly and powerful laymen, and every really important piece of preferment had required political power.

II *The Lottery*

Sydney Smith's writings on the church establishment make clear his view of the economics of a clerical career and explain his sense of absolute justice in pursuing material success in the church through political and social connections. In 1803, he reviewed in the *Edinburgh* Dr. John Sturges' pamphlet, *Thoughts on the Residence of the Clergy*.[3] The occasion of both the pamphlet and the review was the proposed Clergy Residence Act to limit pluralism, the practice by which clergymen drew income from a number of parishes by employing curates to serve in those where they did not reside. Sturges argued that certain legitimate reasons for non-residence be taken into consideration, that the insufficiency of most clerical emoluments required a certain amount of pluralism, and that clergymen occupied away from their parishes in such activities as teaching or serving ministerial functions would suffer a loss of income in being forced to reside without increasing in any way the total service performed by the clergy. Smith endorsed Sturges' views wholeheartedly; and beneath his argument was the assumption that the churchman's right to receive the income of a post he had been appointed to through the usual channels of influence was a right of property, not a salary paid for services rendered. That the claim of a political or clerical public servant on public funds was a species of property was a notion underlying the operation of church and state until late in the nineteenth century. It was accepted as a just and eminently practical view and explains why parliamentary influence and borough nominations could be bought and sold and why the patronage of bishops was often included in their estates and sold to ambitious clergymen by the bishops' heirs.

Smith's views on the payment of the clergy were most fully expressed in his *Letters to Archdeacon Singleton,* published from 1837 to 1839 to protest against certain proposed reforms in church administration.[4] Though he believed that the promise of money should not lure an unqualified man into the clergy, he knew that the prospect of definite poverty could keep many qualified men out. The resources of the Church of England, though large, were unequal to the task of paying all its clergy what they were worth. Unable to pay with money, the church had to pay with promises. Smith compared a clerical career to a lottery in which a few won great prizes and the majority drew blanks. If it was impossible for every clergyman to have income enough to live like an educated English gentleman, then the church had to continue to induce educated gentlemen to accept low salaries in the hopes of some day becoming part of the well-paid hierarchy.

Smith's own career illustrates his theory. He entered the church in order to make his way in the world, and eventually he achieved a high social and material position. Through all his days of poverty, he was an active, intelligent, and effective parson. Had he never become wealthy he would have continued to be just as active, intelligent, and effective. But had the possibility of material success in the church not existed, he might never have become a parson at all.

His theory was Mammonish, but so was the society from which clergymen came, in which they served, and by which they were to be respected—a society which Smith called the "porter-brewing, cotton-spinning, tallow-melting kingdom of Great Britain, bursting with opulence, and flying from poverty as the greatest of human evils." [5]

He was not blind to the disadvantages of the system of promotions and unequal salaries prevalent in the church. The zealous and unmaterialistic clergyman, usually one who neither knew how nor cared to take such actions as would further his career, might be left impoverished for life. The church was one of the very few open roads from the lower-middle class to the gentry traversable in one generation; and with human avidity what it is, the wealth and power of high ecclesiastical office were temptations to the ambitious. Smith described the hypothetical, but typical, rise of a baker's son as follows:

Young Crumpet is sent to school—takes to his books—spends the best years of his life, as all eminent Englishmen do, in making Latin verses —knows that the *crum* in crum-pet is long, and the *pet* short—goes to the University—gets a prize for an Essay on the Dispersion of the Jews—takes orders—becomes a Bishop's chaplain—has a young nobleman for his pupil—publishes an useless classic, and a serious call to the unconverted—and then goes through the Elysian transitions of Prebendary, Dean, Prelate, and the long train of purple, profit, and power.[6]

But despite such abuses, Smith was convinced that the interests of the church would not be better served by a more equal distribution of wealth which would eliminate the great emoluments and inducements at the top without substantially increasing the pittances at the bottom.

Long before the *Letters to Archdeacon Singleton,* Smith had formed and expressed his basic arguments on the system of unequal payment. In 1808, a bill was introduced into Parliament to empower bishops to appoint a curate to any living over five hundred pounds a year and to pay him one-fifth of the income of the vicar. Smith argued against this bill (which was subsequently defeated) in the *Edinburgh Review* and sent some notes to Lord Holland who was to argue against it in the House of Lords.[7] The arguments he offered were that most curates were young gentlemen just out of college, who were serving at meager salaries in low positions while learning their profession and waiting for preferment; that those who were permanent curates and whose curacies were their only subsistence were mostly from the laboring class, without university educations, and were better off financially even at low salaries than they would have been outside the church; that too much power over the lower clergy was already exercised by the bishops; and that there were so few livings over five hundred pounds that the example of injustice to vicars and rectors would have a far greater effect than any general good done for curates.

This distrust of the power of bishops probably stemmed as much from the independent character which Sydney Smith had formed in dealing with his father as it did from his Whiggish suspicion of all centralized and monarchlike authority. "It is a maxim with me," he once wrote, "that a Bishop must always be in the wrong."[8] This maxim governed his views all his life. In 1822, Smith published in the *Edinburgh Review* an article titled "The Bishop of Peterborough and his Clergy."[9] It is so witty and severe an attack on the abuses of episcopal power that when Smith reprinted it in his collected works under the title "Persecuting Bishops," one reader asked whether the word "Bishops" were a nominative or an accusative.

Dr. Herbert Marsh, the Bishop of Peterborough, had compiled a list of eighty-seven questions on matters of faith and theology which he presented to already ordained clergymen. He insisted that they answer the questions briefly and exactly so that he could determine whether their beliefs were free enough from taints of Calvinism for him to admit them as curates in his diocese. Smith's belief that theological distinctions were peripheral to the real

identity of the church brought him to the conclusion that the
Bishop had no right to decide what exact interpretations of the
thirty-nine articles of Anglican faith were orthodox or heretical,
because these were matters for the individual consciences of the
clergymen. He also took this opportunity to parody those staunch
defenders of orthodoxy who, like Bishop Marsh, saw in every
Catholic or dissenter a danger to the establishment of the Church
of England, and who longed to use political and social persecution
as a modern substitute for the stake.

It is inconceivable how such a prelate shakes all the upper works of
the Church, and ripens it for dissolution and decay. Six such Bishops,
multiplied by eighty-seven, and working with five hundred and twenty-
two questions, would fetch everything to the ground in less than six
months. But what if it pleased Divine Providence to afflict every prelate with the spirit of putting eighty-seven queries, and the two Archbishops with the spirit of putting twice as many, and the Bishop of
Sodor and Man with the spirit of putting only forty-three queries?
—there would then be a grand total of two thousand three hundred
and thirty-five interrogations flying about the English Church; and
sorely vexed would the land be with Question and Answer.

Smith's main argument was that the Bishop's examination was
both arbitrary and unjust. However repugnant Calvinistic and
Arminian doctrines were to Bishop Marsh, Smith pointed out,
there was room for them within the tolerant range of orthodox
Anglicanism; but the Bishop had set himself up as the sole arbiter
of orthodoxy and heresy.

A Curate—there is something which excites compassion in the very
name of a Curate!!! How any man of Purple, Palaces, and Preferment,
can let himself loose against this poor working man of God, we are at
a loss to conceive,—a learned man in a hovel, with sermons and sauce-
pans, lexicons and bacon, Hebrew books and ragged children—good
and patient—a comforter and a preacher—the first and purest pauper
in the hamlet, and yet showing, that, in the midst of his worldly misery, he has the heart of a gentleman, and the spirit of a Christian, and
the kindness of a pastor; and this man, though he has exercised the
duties of a clergyman for twenty years—though he has most ample
testimonies of conduct from clergymen as respectable as any Bishop—
though an Archbishop add his name to the list of witnesses, is not good

enough for Bishop Marsh; but is pushed out into the street, with his wife and children, and his little furniture, to surrender his honour, his faith, his conscience, and his learning—or to starve!

III   *Canon of St. Paul's*

Sydney Smith's best known attack on the Bench of Bishops came in the *Letters to Archdeacon Singleton*. The passage of the Reform Bill of 1832 had initiated a program of utilitarian reform in many institutions under government control. Major goals of Church of England reform were the more equal distribution of clerical income and the creation of additional parishes in growing urban areas. An early attempt at such reforms by the Whig government was met with opposition from bishops who threatened to resign if the proposals were pressed. A wiser course of action was taken by the Melbourne government in 1836, when a permanent Ecclesiastical Commission was created by Parliament under a bill introduced by Lord John Russell. The commission consisted of eight laymen, the archbishops of York and Canterbury, and four other bishops, the most energetic and articulate of whom was Charles James Blomfield, Bishop of London.

Certain of the reforms proposed by the Ecclesiastical Commission would have stripped the cathedrals of a good part of their wealth and patronage in order to enrich some small parochial livings and create other new ones—livings which would then come under the patronage of the various episcopal sees. Smith's opposition to these reforms can be easily, if not fairly, called a defense of his own income and patronage, since he was at the time a Canon Residentiary of St. Paul's Cathedral. But his devotion to the interests of St. Paul's, proven by his dedication as a manager of cathedral affairs, was his central motive.

From the beginning of Sydney Smith's tenure at St. Paul's, his talent for practical business was recognized by his colleagues, the other canons and the dean. Chapter-meetings were generally held during the three months a year that Smith was serving his turn conducting divine service at the cathedral and was a resident in London, so that he would be available to execute whatever decisions were made. He undertook all the tasks of inspecting and supervising repairs to the cathedral building; pursuing questions of property, leases, and bequests through law courts; instituting a new system of bill-paying to insure that competitive bids were received before any contracts for work on the cathedral property were given out; installing a system of cisterns and pumps to protect against fire; restoring the library; and taking out fire insurance on the ancient building. When he saw the interests and property of the cathedral threatened once more, not by fire, neglect, mismanagement, or even sight-seeing mobs, but by the Bench of Bishops and the Whig reformers, he took characteristically vigorous and direct action.

From February, 1837, to February, 1839, Smith published three *Letters to Archdeacon Singleton,* addressed to Thomas Singleton, Rector of Howick, Prebendary of Worcester, and Archdeacon of Northumberland, at whose suggestion the pamphlets were written. The *Letters* contain Smith's old arguments against the equal distribution of insufficient funds and for the lottery system of unequal payments, as well as attacks on the Ecclesiastical Commission itself for giving the bishops the right to make decisions for, about, and in the name of the entire clergy without any representation of the lower ranks of the church. In addition, he is suspicious of the Whig reformers, who had just achieved a victory over the centralized authority of the Crown and nobles apparently in order to establish a new centralized authority of commissions and bureaus.

The Whig Government, they will be vexed to hear, would find a great deal of patronage forced upon them by this measure. Their favorite human animal, the Barrister of six years' standing, would be called into action. The whole earth is, in fact, in commission, and the human race saved from the Flood are delivered over to Barristers of six years' standing. The *onus probandi* now lies upon any man who says he is not a Commissioner; the only doubt on seeing a new man among the Whigs is, not whether he is a Commissioner or not, but whether it is Tithes, Poor Laws, Boundaries of Boroughs, Church Leases, Charities, or any of the thousand human concerns which are now worked by Commissioners.[10]

The work is typical of Smith's wittiest and sharpest polemical style, not only full of logical arguments but also, in *Edinburgh Review* fashion, offering numerous *ad hominem* attacks on the commissioners. The bishops, Smith frequently points out, did not extend their generosity with cathedral property to redistributing episcopal income and patronage.

The Bishops and Commissioners wanted a fund to endow small Livings; they did not touch a farthing of their own incomes, only distributed them a little more equally; and proceeded lustily at once to confiscate Cathedral property. But why was it necessary, if the fund for small Livings was such a paramount consideration, that the future Archbishops of Canterbury should be left with two palaces, and 15,000*l.* per annum? Why is every future Bishop of London to have a palace in Fulham, a house in St. James's Square, and 10,000*l.* a year?

He goes on to imagine the inevitable moment when the bishops will be informed that, having turned cathedral property over to the commission, their own incomes and patronage will also be taken over by government. "The Commission was separated in an instant: London clenched his fist; Canterbury was hurried out by his chaplains, and put into a warm bed; a solemn vacancy spread itself over the face of Gloucester; Lincoln was taken out in strong hysterics." [11]

Smith's close acquaintance with the Whig aristocracy also enabled him to caricature the political commissioners with telling accuracy. Of the Home Secretary, originator of the Ecclesiastical Commission and Smith's own long-time friend, he says:

There is not a better man in England than Lord John Russell; but his worst failure is that he is utterly ignorant of all moral fear; there is nothing he would not undertake. I believe he would perform the operation for the stone—build St. Peter's—or assume (with or without ten minutes' notice) the command of the Channel Fleet; and no one would discover by his manner that the patient had died—the Church tumbled down—and the Channel Fleet been knocked to atoms.[12]

And in a brilliant paragraph, he captures Viscount Melbourne, the Prime Minister, who disguised very shrewd and professional statesmanship behind the aristocratic mask of blasé indifference and amateurish politics.

Instead of this lofty nebulo, this miracle of moral and intellectual felicities, he is nothing more than a sensible honest man, who means to do his duty to the Sovereign and to the Country; instead of being the ignorant man he pretends to be, before he meets the deputation of Tallow-Chandlers in the morning, he sits up half the night talking with Thomas Young about melting and skimming, and then, though he has acquired knowledge enough to work off a whole vat of prime Leicester tallow, he pretends next morning not to know the difference between a dip and a mould. In the same way, when he has been employed in reading Acts of Parliament, he would persuade you that he has been reading *Cleghorn on the Beatitudes,* or *Pickler on the Nine Difficult Points.*[13]

In January, 1838, Smith noted that his first pamphlet had had some success. "I see by the Report of the Church Commissioners of December last all the points for which the Cathedrals contended are given up. This is very handsome on the part of the Commissioners," he wrote to Lady Grey, "and their reform whether wise or not will at least be just." [14] Yet at the same time he was preparing his second *Letter to Archdeacon Singleton,* questioning the wisdom of the commission's proposals and the justice of its representation of the clergy. Lady Holland wrote on February 17, 1838, "Sydney Smith is going to publish another attack upon the Church Commission. To be sure the *mischief is done* by his former publication; but he is shutting the door closer to a Bishopric. . . . with all his wit & talents, he is woefully deficient in tacte [*sic*]." [15]

But by 1838 Smith was convinced that the door to a bishopric was already securely closed against him, and his attack on the Ecclesiastical Commissioners was, if anything, prompted by a sense of injury rather than by a lack of tact. Smith had always expected that the return of the Whigs to office would result in his being offered a bishopric and the opportunity to take an active part in government in the only place allowed an Anglican clergyman, on the Bench of Bishops in the House of Lords. By 1830, when his chances of being raised to episcopal rank first became possible, Smith had already decided that his age and health would not allow him to carry out the duties of a bishopric, but he still felt that his devotion to the Whigs and their liberal opinions throughout the long years of opposition should at least be recognized by an offer, even if he fully intended to decline the mitre. In 1834, Lord Holland remarked that he thought a recent episcopal choice had been a poor one and that Samuel Butler would have been his own candidate. This so offended Smith that he wrote a series of letters to Holland House, asking why his old friend had not done him the courtesy of even mentioning him. "If the See of Bristol had been offered to me nothing would have induced me to take it—there is scarcely any Bishopric I *would* take; but I think I do not deserve the disgrace from my party of being past over and the dignity never offered me." [16]

The Whigs of the Grey and Melbourne cabinets knew that Smith had offended the high-church Anglicans by his writings in defense of Catholics and the low-church Anglicans by his attacks on evangelicalism. In the midst of an extensive reform program, reaching even into the church itself, they could not afford to alienate the clergy by rewarding properly the one clergyman who had stood by them for so many years. Lord John Russell wrote that if it had been up to him, Smith should have had the opportunity to decline a mitre, and Lord Melbourne admitted in later years that he regretted nothing in his career more than not having made Smith a bishop. But these confidences were made in private correspondence; publicly, the politicians could or would do nothing for Sydney Smith.

Another factor that outweighed Smith's merits was his reputation as a wit and joker. Macaulay noted on June 7, 1831:

Sydney Smith leaves London on the 20th, the day before Parliament meets for business. I advised him to stay, and see something of his friends who would be crowding to London. "My flock!" said this good shepherd. "My dear Sir, remember my flock!
      The hungry sheep look up and are not fed."
I could say nothing to such an argument; but I could not help thinking that, if Mr. Daniel Wilson had said such a thing, it would infallibly have appeared in his funeral sermon, and in his Life by Baptist Noel. But in poor Sydney's mouth it sounded like a joke.[17]

Smith recognized the fact that people refused to take him seriously. In a letter to Bishop Blomfield of London, published in *The Times* as part of the running controversy between the two churchmen over church reform, Smith says, "You call me in [your] speech your facetious friend, and I hasten with gratitude in this letter to denominate you my solemn friend; but you and I must not run into commonplace errors; you must not think me necessarily foolish because I am facetious, nor will I consider you necessarily wise because you are grave." [18]

IV *An Instrument for Teaching Religion*

Despite Sydney Smith's witticisms in dealing with matters of the church visible, his own faith was simple and firm. He took the gospels as a true record of the life and teachings of Jesus Christ, intended to show man the way to live a moral life in order to earn a heavenly reward. Sharing this faith with his parishioners meant, to him, teaching them morality and helping them to enjoy the bounty of Providence.

Smith thought that a national church had a necessary function in society, though this function was not to express a particular doctrine. In a sermon on toleration, first delivered in 1807, he says, "The church must be distinguished from religion itself. . . . A church establishment is only an instrument for teaching religion; but an instrument of admirable contrivance and vast utility." In order to maintain such an establishment, he goes on, a clergy must be educated to teach Christianity on the basis of sound historical and scriptural learning and must be paid by a compulsory levy on all the people so that it is independent of any influence from individuals. Articles of faith must be established so that doctrine, throughout the church, is a matter of accepted assurance and not a subject of controversy.[19]

The function of doctrine in an established church, then, according to Smith, is to afford a definition of belief which will form the basis of that moral instruction which is the church's primary task. Any church which teaches men to follow the precepts of Christ and to have faith in Him as their Saviour is a Christian church and can guide its members in Christian living. Smith says in another place, "The true Christian, amid all the diversities of opinion, searches for the holy in desire, for the good in council, for the just in works; and he loves the good, under whatever temple, at whatever altar he may find them."

Yet, along with this evident latitudinarianism, he also states that "The Church of England is the wisest and most enlightened sect of Christians." [20] It seems obvious that one sect can be superior to another, not because of a difference in theology, but because its articles of faith are flexible enough and at the same time well enough established to allow its ministers to teach, calmly and assuredly, the Christian morality without undue stress on matters of theology or faith. This view of Smith's largely explains his attack on the narrow orthodoxy of Bishop Marsh of Peterborough. And since he regarded the privileged position of the established church as due not to the particular theology which separated it from other sects but to the social and moral functions which united it to them, he saw nothing to fear from the political strength of non-Anglicans. Therefore, he had no sympathy with the discriminatory laws against Catholics and dissenters which the overwhelming majority of his colleagues supported so vigorously.

Smith's teaching of religion, like his views on payment of the clergy, made allowances for the weaknesses of human nature and the limitations which practice placed upon ideal theory. Late in his career he said, "I have always avoided speculative, and preached practical, religion." [21] The principles which he thought should govern the preaching of "practical" religion he set down in 1801 in the preface to an early volume of his sermons.

The clergy are allowed about twenty-six hours every year for the instruction of their fellow-creatures; and I cannot help thinking that this short time had better be employed on practical subjects, in explaining and enforcing that conduct which the spirit of Christianity requires, and which mere worldly happiness commonly coincides to recommend. . . . Critical explanations of difficult passages of Scripture, learned investigations of the meaning and accomplishment of the prophecies, do well for publication, but are ungenial to the habits and tastes of a general audience. Of the highest importance they are to those who can defend the faith and study it profoundly; but, God forbid it should be necessary to be a scholar, or a critic, in order to be a Christian. [22]

Smith carried this principle into practice. The great bulk of the sermons he delivered, those given on innumerable Sundays to the country parishioners of Foston and Combe Florey, from 1809 until his death, no longer exist. The sermons which he published were selected from those preached at various metropolitan private chapels or institutions or on special occasions from such pulpits as Bristol Cathedral, St. Paul's, and the Cathedral Church

of St. Peter, in York. Yet even before cosmopolitan, educated society, where a leavening of theological or exegetical discourse
would be expected, Smith tended to make his sermons predomi-
nantly moralistic. He lays down clear rules for the Christian life,
stressing the responsibility of Christians to do good to their fellow
men, to act upon sound principles, and to maintain a calm and
rational faith in God's limitless benevolence. He almost never
dwells upon the spiritual acts which the Christian is called upon
to perform. In a sermon on the death of Christ, he speaks of the
last days and the crucifixion as "fit subjects for examination, either
as they afford an additional example of the truth of the Christian
religion, or a practical example of morality." [23] The sermon goes
on to find in the story of the Passion a lesson of bravery, calmness,
forgiveness, and firmness. The doctrine of vicarious atonement is
not mentioned, and Christ is referred to as "the founder of our
religion" as well as "our Saviour." It seems reasonable to assume
that Smith's parochial preaching was even more moralistic and
less theological.

In a sermon "On the Love of Country," Smith justified his
emphasis on moralism. "An attempt is often made," he says, "to
distinguish between moral and Christian subjects of investigation;
but . . . there is no action of our lives which concerns the interests of others, in which we do not either violate or obey a Christian law; I cannot, therefore, illustrate a moral duty, without, at
the same time, enforcing a precept of our religion." Even in dealing with so strictly spiritual a subject as "The Utility of Meditat-
ing on Death," Smith found an opportunity for moral instruction.
"One great advantage of the meditation on death is, that it teaches
us to value all earthly things aright; and perpetually corrects the
fallacy of our calculations, by reminding us of the period to which
they apply;—it discourages those schemes of fraud, injustice and
ambition, the fruits of which are distant, by reminding us, that
that distance we may never reach,—that death, which cuts short
the enjoyment, leaves us with the whole load of guilt."

There is an implicit materialism in sermons which stress good
works as the reason and basis of a Christian life rather than as
fruits of a life rooted in Christian faith. The materialism becomes
explicit when religious teaching, as Smith's very often does, pleads
for a higher standard of human conduct by pointing out the re-

sults of morality, not in laying up treasures in heaven, but in improving life on earth. For example, in a sermon "On Truth," Smith says, "Upon truth rests all human knowledge; to truth man is indebted for the hourly preservation of his life, and for a perpetual guide to his actions; without truth the affairs of the world would no longer exist, as they now are, than they could if any of the great physical laws of the universe were suspended."

Or again, in a sermon "On the Treatment of Servants," he says, "There is one very striking advantage in this amiable behaviour to our domestics for those who are engaged in the truly noble occupation of gradually correcting and improving their characters; it affords a constant exercise for the virtues of justice and moderation, and it is in the bosom of their families, and in the midst of those who are the daily witnesses of their actions, that men ought to render virtue habitual to themselves."

The first of these passages seems to imply that truth is important to man because upon it depend worldly affairs; the second, that humane treatment of one's servants is valuable as an object lesson in virtue for one's children. These are sound but not particularly Christian arguments.

Sydney Smith was convinced that theological understanding had to be achieved on an intellectual level far above that of the great mass of his parishioners. Speculative or metaphysical sermons could only bore and drive away his listeners, or at best confuse them. The only other way in which the lower classes could be led to an appreciation of the profounder mysteries of faith was that of mystical enthusiasts, who exploited emotional experiences and stressed supernatural influences on everyday life. Rather than fall into the hollow spirituality he believed was being spread by evangelicalism, he chose to run the risk of seeming to be materialistic in an attempt to exemplify and justify Christian living to his congregations by showing them its actions and effects in their daily lives.

Since Sydney Smith saw his pulpit as a place from which to teach morality, public as well as private, he had no scruples about using it as a political platform. A number of his sermons deal with the same issues he had written on in pamphlets and in the *Edinburgh Review* and contain the same arguments. In 1807, he preached and published a sermon "On Toleration," decrying the spirit of persecution prevalent in the country and refuting the current arguments against giving political equality to the Roman Catholics. During that same summer, his *Letters of Peter Plymley* started appearing on the same subjects. Many years later, in 1828, when Catholic emancipation was once again an important political issue, he preached a sermon on toleration to the Mayor and Corporation of Bristol at a special Guy Fawkes Day service, traditionally an occasion for anti-Catholic harangues.[24]

On March 28, 1824, he preached a sermon on "The Judge that Smites Contrary to the Law" before two justices of the King's Bench, during the York assizes.[25] Preaching on the ideal principle of British common law, "Equal rights to unequal possessions, equal justice to the rich and poor," Smith echoed in this sermon his arguments for reform of abuses in the criminal code, arguments which had been contained in two *Edinburgh Review* articles, one on the Game Laws and one on abusive treatment of poor prisoners, which had appeared only a few months before. In a "Sermon on the Duties of the Queen," delivered in St. Paul's soon after the accession of Victoria, Smith set out to "take a short review of the moral and religious state of the country," and in so doing urged the young monarch to educate the poor, avoid war, and promote religious toleration.[26] For he preached the morality of government as well as the morality of private life, and speaking of the importance of public worship, he said:

The public worship of God is the ancient, and the sure guardian of human happiness:—do not trifle with it as if it were of no avail; justice, and faith, and mercy, and kindness, flow from the altars of God,—it is here that men learn to pity;—it is here that they are taught to forgive;—it is here that they learn punctuality in contracts, obedience to magistrates, submission to superiors, respect for laws, loyalty to kings; and there, above all, it is, that they catch that true spirit of the Gospel, which, meliorating all things, makes submission to superiors voluntary, by rendering superiors gracious,—respect for the laws natural, by making laws just,—the loyalty to kings pleasant, by making kings good.[27]

The style of Sydney Smith's sermons is appropriate to their purpose. In general, his discourses are carefully reasoned arguments whose major literary merits are clarity and coherence. He starts his sermon "On Dissipation," for example, with the statement, "In the progress of society, fresh crimes, follies, and virtues, as well as new sciences, and arts, emerge into notice; and to study mankind aright, we must observe, no less the circumstances in which he is placed, than the feelings, passions, and talents, of which he is composed." The sermon goes on to examine self-indulgence, from its origins in the leisure brought about by civilization to its evil effects on both spiritual and material welfare.

Smith uses such step-by-step logic rather than striking imagery, because he wants to appeal to the reason and not the emotions of his hearers. When he does use a simile or a metaphor, he generally does so to reinforce some example or illustration of a moral principle. He tells his congregation to preserve their attachment to morality for its own sake "as the children of Israel preserved the ark, and the seraphim kept the gates of Paradise." [28] He speaks of making restitution for injuries as a necessary first step toward repentance. "If seas and mountains separate us from the being we have injured, we should pass over mountains and seas to find him; to beg his prayers to God, and to restore him wine, and oil, and vineyards, and oliveyards, tenfold for all we have taken." [29]

He did not restrict himself to the Bible as a source of imagery. "There is a bad taste in the language of sermons," he once said, "evinced by a constant repetition of the same scriptural phrases, which perhaps were used with great judgment two hundred years ago, but are now become so trite that they may, without any great detriment, be exchanged for others." [30] He preferred to use images from everyday life to drive his lesson home to his parishioners, as when he argues against those who complain of the irksomeness of regular attendance at worship by pointing to the irksome tasks undertaken in the name of professional duty. "Who rejects the most loathsome disease? who shrinks from the driest forms of the Law? who turns away in disgust from the dullest calculations?—The mammon of unrighteousness can infuse into us all a meekness and patience which we are slow to feel in the service of our God." [31] When he had occasion to appeal to the emotions, avoiding the usual Biblical phrases, he could construct imagery on a Homeric scale. In a sermon "For the Scotch Lying-in Hospital," he speaks of the sun, hastening onwards to other climates, to carry to all tongues, and people, and nations the splendour of day. . . . It will beam upon the savage and sensual Moor; it will lighten the robber of Arabia to his prey; it will glitter on the chains of the poor negro. It will waken the Indian of the ocean to eat the heart of his captive. The bigot Turk will hail it from the summit of his mosque; it will guide the Brahmin to his wooden gods; but in all its course it will witness perhaps no other spectacle of a free, rational people, gathered together under the influence of Revelation, to lighten the load of human misery, and to give of their possessions to the afflicted, and the poor.

But for the most part, his use of imagery is strictly subservient to his logic, and his emphasis is always on the immediate and the practical. Though his flights and figures may be aimed at moving a congregation to charity, he always returns to logical and even prosaic argument to win conviction.

There is a charity which originates from the romantic fiction of humble virtue and innocence in distress; but this will be soon disgusted by low artifice, and scared by brutal vice. The charity which proceeds from ostentation can exist no longer than when its motives remain undetected. There is . . . a charity which is meant to excite the feelings of gratitude, but this will meet with its termination in disappointment. That charity alone endures, which flows from a sense of duty, and a hope in God.[32]

Sydney Smith applied his own standards to the sermons of others when criticizing them in the *Edinburgh Review*. In reviewing *Discourses on Various Subjects*, a volume of sermons by Thomas Rennel, Smith complains of the lack of imaginative novelty which characterizes this addition to the mass of barren English pulpit oratory, "in which the weary Christian can descry nothing around him but a dreary expanse of trite sentiments and languid words." [33] The only sermon of Rennel's which Smith applauds is one on gambling, a strongly moralistic one like Smith's own. In the same number of the *Edinburgh*, Smith reviewed a sermon by Robert Nares, and found it wanting, also. Nares' offense was straying beyond the bounds of logical moralizing to warn that a recent bad harvest was a direct punishment by Providence of greedy corn merchants. "So that the Archdeacon [Nares], after denying that any body knows *when, how*, and *why* the Creator works a miracle, proceeds to specify the *time, instrument,* and *object* of a miraculous scarcity. . . ." [34] To reinforce morality by calling down the direct interference of the Deity was not only contrary to Smith's bent for logical argument but was also, in his opinion, a dangerous sort of precedent to set for superstitious people too easily led by emotions into mistaking their prejudices for divine inspirations.

Because he considered the church as the state's instrument for teaching religion, Smith looked with disfavor on amateur moralists who tried to enforce morality by social pressure or legislation. In 1809, Smith reported in the *Edinburgh Review* on the activities of the Society for the Suppression of Vice, a private subscription organization formed for the purpose of detecting and bringing to trial violators of such laws as existed to curb immorality, bans on bull- and bear-baiting, sabbath-breaking, and the like.[35] A secondary purpose of the Society was to revive other moralistic laws which had not been enforced for many years. Smith points out that the effect of such private societies could be the weakening of public authorities established to enforce the law; and he goes on, with mock gravity, to ask whether there should be private societies organized to gather foreign intelligence, transport criminals, supply the army and navy, or supervise woods and forests. In a more serious vein, he questions the ability of either public or private groups to legislate morality. "You may drag men into church by main force, and prosecute them for buying a pot of beer,—and cut them off from the enjoyment of a leg of mutton;—and you may do all this, till you make the common people hate Sunday, and the clergy, and religion, and every thing which related to such subjects."

Smith's most telling points in the essay are made against the implicit hypocrisy of such an organization which, consisting only of Church of England members of the upper class, "should denominate themselves a Society for suppressing the vices of persons whose income does not exceed 500*l. per annum;* and then, to put all classes upon an equal footing, there must be another society of barbers, butchers, and bakers, to return to the higher classes that moral character, by which they are so highly benefited." The Society acts vigorously to eliminate the bear-baiting of the artisan, but sees no objection to its own members engaging in angling, which Smith calls, "Running an iron hook in the intestines of an animal; presenting this first animal to another as his food; and then pulling this second animal up and suspending him by the barb in his stomach"; or in hunting, which Smith defines as, "Riding a horse till he drops, in order to see an innocent animal torn to pieces by dogs." Drinking and gambling are vices to the Society when they find the workman at his ale and cockfight, but not when they find the gentleman at his wine and cards.

A second, and much later, article by Smith dealing with the impracticality and unfairness of trying to legislate away the immorality of the lower classes, was one he wrote in 1826 on the "Licensing of Alehouses." [36] In both articles it seems that Smith was ahead of his time in seeing that drinking and other vices of the poor were more a result of their impoverished condition than a cause; and he speaks of these vices as inevitable outlets of the brutality of working-class life.

V   A Conscience Active, Clear, and Just

The *Edinburgh Review* for October, 1803, contained Sydney Smith's review of Jacques Necker's *Cours de Morale Religieuse*. Necker, a former French statesman exiled in Switzerland, wrote this work as a series of lay sermons intended to give the French people a religious ethic to fill the moral void left by the Revolution's destruction of the church. One of Smith's comments on Necker is particularly interesting in that it contains a criticism of the kind later often leveled against Smith himself. "He appears indeed to have assumed the Christian character, rather from a sense of its utility or expediency [in teaching morality], than from a conviction of its truth; and his sermons are to be considered as deistical essays written in a Christian country." [37]

This comment seems to be echoed in an article on Smith which could only say of his preaching, at best, that "As a supplement to the essence of Christian preaching, Mr. Smith's sermons were admirable." [38] More violent opinions called his moralism a brand of religion "which lets the conscience sleep, while the heart is unchanged." [39] Perhaps the fairest summary of Smith's religious career was that in the *Christian Observer*, published ten years after Smith's death. The article points out that Smith lacked the kind of spirituality necessary for the highest type of religious life and says that men like him, who despite sound principles are confined in their thinking to this world, "are satisfied with things as they exist; or at most they desire to mend this world: they do not realize its emptiness; they do not set their hearts on another. But in compensation, may we say, they are gifted with a conscience active, clear, and just, within their circumscribed range of vision." Such a conscience, the writer goes on, results in a sense of duty, of social obligation, and of God as the giver of the moral law within one's heart.[40]

This is just, but to judge Sydney Smith as unfit for the clergy on these grounds is to ignore the differences between late eighteenth-century and mid-Victorian views of the clergy. Smith's idea of religion was closely akin to the notions of his political and social associates. Charles James Fox said in Parliament, in 1791, that "the religious establishment of any country was to be governed not so much with regard to the purity of the precepts and truth of a religion, as with a view to that sort of religion which was most likely to inculcate morality and religion in the minds." [41] A recent historian says, "When men spoke of 'the Whig religion,' in terms which suggested a collective outlook, they implied a creed intensely protestant, but bereft of three of the principal characteristics of seventeenth-century Puritanism—zeal, dogma, and anti-Popish politics." [42]

Before the Oxford Movement and evangelicalism laid greater stress on dogma and liturgy than eighteenth-century English Protestantism had known, before Parliamentary reforms and private societies increased extra-ecclesiastical education and welfare activities, the Church of England maintained in each parish a priest to look after the minds and bodies, as well as the souls, of his congregation. In this context, there was need for secular clergymen like Sydney Smith, kind, active, educated, gentlemen of the church such as are encountered in the novels of Jane Austen.

While Sydney Smith was still a young curate, he established a Sunday school for the poor children of Netheravon. Not content with providing spelling books, testaments, and tracts, he arranged for comfortable schoolrooms and warm clothing for the ill-clad pupils. He was an amateur physician, having studied some medicine in college and having attended medical lectures later;

and besides examining and treating his parishioners at Foston and Combe Florey, he kept an apothecary's shop in his rectory from which he dispensed free medications of all kinds to the villagers, for whom regular medical care was often unobtainable and always expensive. He was concerned about the meager diet of the poor and constantly experimented with various foods, stuffing hungry workmen with rice, broth, or porridge, trying to develop a nutritious diet cheaper than the bread on which the laboring class lived almost exclusively. He established small individual gardens for his parishioners on his unused land, so that they would be able to grow some vegetables to vary their diet and would be partially independent of the uncertain wheat crop.

It was not only by caring for their health that Sydney Smith went beyond his minimal ceremonial duties in bringing Christian precept and example into the homes of his parishioners. He considered visiting the poor and sick a necessary part of the constant education of a clergyman as well as a sacred obligation. "He who only knows the misfortunes of mankind at second hand, and by description," he preached, "has but a faint idea of what is really suffered in the world." [43] He took up the office of Justice of the Peace in Yorkshire more as a reformer of morals and a protector of the ignorant than as a harsh judge over petty offenders. His parishes had good reason for thinking of their church as an active force in their lives and of religion as a seven-days-a-week way of life.

CHAPTER 3

Papists, Politics, and Peter Plymley

I *The Catholic Controversy*

WHEN Pitt died in January, 1806, George III lost the only man capable of leading an all-Tory government and had to call upon Lord Grenville, leader of the conservative Whigs, to form a coalition cabinet. Grenville insisted, over the King's objections, on making Charles James Fox Secretary of State for Foreign Affairs and Leader of Commons. It was Fox who was the real leader of this so-called Ministry of All the Talents, and he set two major tasks for himself—the abolition of the slave trade and the establishment of peace with France. The first was accomplished, but peace remained elusive and all chances vanished with Fox's death in September, 1806.

Lord Grenville tried to shore up his collapsing government by turning attention from the diplomatic fiasco to a domestic issue. Convinced that Napoleon would try to invade Ireland and turn the dissatisfied Irish into allies against England, he wanted to start removing the restrictions which kept Roman Catholics from holding public office. His government introduced, therefore, a bill to admit Catholics to staff rank in the army. The question of Catholic emancipation was not a new one and had been supported at various times by almost all the leading statesmen of both Whig and Tory affiliation, Pitt, Castlereagh, and Canning as well as Fox and Grey. But the King became indignant at this affront to one of his favorite prejudices and insisted that his ministers not only drop the bill but give him their promise never to introduce such a measure again. Unwilling, and indeed unable, to continue in office under such a restriction, the cabinet resigned on March 18, 1807.

The King found in the Duke of Portland a leader willing to accept office under a pledge of continued anti-Catholic legislation, and Portland quickly surrounded himself with a number of followers of second-rate abilities but unquestioned loyalty to the Crown. In the general election that followed, the Tory government went to the people with cries of "No-Popery" and "Protect the Church and King" and won a substantial victory at the polls.

The fall of the Grenville cabinet and the resulting political alignments brought a religious question to the forefront of political argument for the first time in many years. Sydney Smith was the perfect man for the moment, able to argue on an issue of church and state with the kind of wit and insight that Swift had displayed on such topics a century earlier. Shortly after the installation of the Portland government, Smith preached a sermon on toleration at Temple Church. He published the sermon with a preface that says, in part:

Charity towards those who dissent from us on religious opinions is always a proper subject for the pulpit. If such discussions militate against the views of any particular party, the fault is not in him who is thus erroneously said to introduce politics into the Church, but in those who have really brought the Church into politics. It does not cease to be our duty to guard men against religious animosities, . . . because intolerance has lately been made the road to power.[1]

The sermon itself carefully avoids any political arguments and deals with Catholic emancipation only as it affects the church establishment. An established church, Smith argues, is publicly supported in order to assure the teaching of religion in the nation; its tenets distinguish it from other sects but are not the reason for its privileged position. Dissent from Anglican worship, therefore, is not tantamount to plotting the overthrow of the Church of England. Smith goes on to point out, in refutation, that the cruelties practiced by the Catholic Church during the Inquisition or the reign of "Bloody" Mary were not characteristic of the Catholic religion but of the barbaric period during which the Church of Rome was dominant and seeking to curb dissent; and he argues that the nineteenth-century Catholic is no more responsible for the savagery of the past than the nineteenth-century Protestant is responsible for the cruelties of Elizabeth.[2]

When Smith wrote on Catholic emancipation in the *Edinburgh Review,* he attacked the political, rather than the religious, side of the question. In a review of William Parnell's *Historical Apol-*

ogy for the Irish Catholics, Smith said that unless the claims of the Catholics to civil equity were met, Ireland would join Napoleon in destroying England, church establishment and all; that the animosity of the Irish Catholics was due more to a long history of persecution by the English than to religious differences; and that the real reason for the Tories' insistence on keeping Catholics from full citizenship was to pamper the prejudices of George III and stay in office.[3]

II *Brother Peter and Brother Abraham*

Sydney Smith's fullest treatment of the Catholic question and probably his most enduring contribution to the Whig cause was neither a sermon nor a review. During the summer of 1807, which the Smith family spent in the country village of Sonning, there was published the first of a series of four pamphlets entitled *Letters on the Subject of the Catholics, to My Brother Abraham, Who Lives in the Country,* under the nom de plume of Peter Plymley. The fourth pamphlet appeared in early 1808, and by the end of that year the *Peter Plymley Letters,* comprising ten letters in all, had run through at least eleven, and possibly as many as sixteen, editions. Its immense popularity resisted the passage of time, and in 1838, a year before Smith published it in his collected works, Longmans brought out a twenty-first edition. Such tremendous sales, considering the unpopularity of the cause, were amazing. Archibald Constable, who had a keen eye for markets, once estimated the chances of commercial success for a pamphlet as being, at that time, one in a thousand.

Smith's authorship of the *Peter Plymley Letters* was, from the first, an open secret. At the time, his penchant for conspiratorial secrecy, which had prompted him in Edinburgh to insist on backstairs meetings when the *Edinburgh Review* was being planned, led him to ask his friends, in an only half-joking manner, to keep his secret. When he finally acknowledged the work, in publishing it among his collected essays, he stated that, "The Government of that day took great pains to find out the author; all that they *could* find was, that they were brought to Mr. Budd, the publisher, by the Earl of Lauderdale." [4] This statement must be an exaggeration, for there is no evidence that the government made any attempt to prove authorship or to sue for seditious libel;

and as there are many references in various contemporary accounts to Smith's identity as Peter Plymley, there seems to have been little room for doubt.

The main arguments of the *Peter Plymley Letters* are few in number and frequently repeated. Smith's central point is that England, threatened with total destruction by Napoleon, cannot afford to have a disaffected island off her western shore. He points out the growing wealth and strength of the Irish Catholics, whom English persecution has made enemies rather than allies. This threat to national security is the major weapon which Smith uses to arouse sympathy for the Catholic cause. His second point is an appeal to national justice, and he argues that the restrictions placed on Roman Catholics are an abridgment of liberty not at all justified by whatever small danger Catholic officeholders may present to the establishment of the Church of England.

A good part of the *Peter Plymley Letters* is devoted to refutation of the arguments put forth by the "No-Popery" faction and to ridicule of the real, selfish motives of those most vocal in opposing the Catholic claims for equality. The Church of England must indeed be weak, he says, if it can be disestablished by the handful of Catholic peers and commoners who would enter Parliament should the laws against them be relaxed. Nothing could be more foolish, he argues, than to distrust the honor of the Catholic or to impeach his respect of an oath, when the only thing which keeps the Catholic out of office is his refusal to take an oath denying his faith and affirming the religious supremacy of the King. The violent persecution of early Protestants, Smith affirms, is not a crime to be imputed to modern Catholics but to be attributed to the barbarity of the times during which the Catholic Church was defending its establishment.

For the real motives for continued discrimination against the Catholics in an age when religious issues should no longer affect political life, Smith points to the smug superiority of the people in general and the hypocritical demagoguery of those politicians who keep their hands in the public treasury by inflaming public hatred. All the devices of ridicule and opprobrium which Smith had developed to excoriate authors in the *Edinburgh Review* he uses against the Portland ministers who had come into office on a policy of religious persecution.

His chief targets are Spencer Perceval, Chancellor of the Exchequer and the real head of Portland's government, and George Canning, the ex-Foxite who had thrown his lot in with the Pittites and held the office of Secretary of State for Foreign Affairs. Perceval, like the King, was known as a sober family man of deep (though evangelical) religious conviction. To Smith, this appearance of virtue was ridiculous, in view of Perceval's getting a lion's share of the public treasury, "having secured for his own eating and drinking, and the eating and drinking of the Master and Miss Percevals, the reversionary sum of 21,000*l.* a year of the public money, and having just failed in a desperate and rapacious attempt to secure to himself for life the revenues of the Duchy of Lancaster." [5]

The picture of Perceval that Smith draws is that of a smooth-faced hypocrite, willing to risk disaster and violence in order to flatter the prejudices of a senile king and keep place, power, and wealth.

I cannot describe the horror and disgust which I felt at hearing Mr. Perceval call upon the then ministry for measures of vigour in Ireland. If I lived at Hampstead upon stewed meats and claret; if I walked to church every Sunday before eleven young gentlemen of my own begetting, with their faces washed, and their hair pleasingly combed; if the Almighty had blessed me with every earthly comfort,—how awfully would I pause before I sent forth the flame and the sword over the cabins of the poor, brave, generous, open-hearted peasants of Ireland! [6]

George Canning's reputation as a wit, acquired mainly from dinner-table conversations, Parliamentary sallies, and squibs in the *Anti-Jacobin Review,* becomes in Smith's hand a weapon against him.

Providence has made him a light, jesting, paragraph-writing man, and that he will remain to his dying day. When he is jocular he is strong, when he is serious he is like Sampson [sic] in a wig: . . . call him a legislator, a reasoner, and the conductor of the affairs of a nation, and it seems to me as absurd as if a butterfly were to teach bees to make honey. . . . He is a fly in amber, nobody cares about the fly: the only question is, How the Devil did it get there? [7]

[61]

Other Tory ministers, Lord Mulgrave, Lord Hawkesbury, Lord Castlereagh, and Lord Sidmouth, are treated in a similar though more perfunctory manner. Smith can sum up his contempt for a government which bases its policy on religious intolerance with a piece of bitter irony reflective of Swift. He proposes that some dissenting sect far less numerous and powerful than the Catholics be selected for the systematic persecution apparently necessary to the self-esteem of the Anglican. "Why torture a bull-dog, when you can get a frog or a rabbit? I am sure my proposal will meet with the most universal approbation. Do not be apprehensive of any opposition from ministers. If it is a case of hatred, we are sure that one man will defend it by the Gospel: if it abridges human freedom, we know that another will find precedents for it in the Revolution." [8]

Violent abuse was not the only device which Smith carried over from his *Edinburgh Review* writing to pamphlets. Just as his facility for whipping authors is expanded, in the longer work, to vilify political opponents, his gift for witty metaphor and simile becomes, when writ large, a turn for effective analogy. When he finds historical parallels to suit his purpose, he uses them skillfully. He cites the example of Scotland to show that religious freedom has, in the past, changed a rebellious people into a loyal part of the kingdom. He points out that by giving Protestants equality with Catholics in Hungary, Austria was able to unite its people to resist Napoleon and that the Catholic establishment there has survived both the admission of non-Catholics to public office and the onslaughts of the French. By expanding the image and developing details, Smith is able to take even such a worn metaphor as the "ship of state" and make it lively and effective. He pictures England as a frigate under attack by a corsair and in danger of destruction. As for the Captain, Perceval by name,

the first thing he does is to secure 20 or 30 of his prime sailors who happen to be Catholics, to clap them in irons, and set over them a guard of as many Protestants; having taken this admirable method of defending himself against his infidel opponents, he goes upon deck, reminds the sailors, in a very bitter harangue, that they are of different religions; exhorts the Episcopal gunner not to trust the Presbyterian quarter-master; issues positive orders that the Catholics should be fired at upon the first appearance of discontent; rushes through blood and brains, examining his men in the Catechism and 39 Articles, and positively forbids every one to sponge or ram who has not taken the Sacrament according to the Church of England. . . . And built as she is of heart of oak, and admirably manned, is it possible with such a captain, to save this ship from going to the bottom? [9]

When neither precedent nor metaphor serves his purpose, Smith turns to his own inventiveness to put his opponents in the most ridiculous light.

There is a village (no matter where) in which the inhabitants, on one day in the year, sit down to a dinner prepared at the common expense; by an extraordinary piece of tyranny (which Lord Hawkesbury would call the wisdom of the village ancestors), the inhabitants of three of the streets, about a hundred years ago, seized upon the inhabitants of the fourth street, bound them hand and foot, laid them upon their backs, and compelled them to look on while the rest were stuffing themselves with beef and beer: the next year the inhabitants of the persecuted street (though they contributed an equal quota of the expense) were treated precisely in the same manner. The tyranny grew into a custom; and (as the manner of our nature is) it was considered as the most sacred of all duties to keep these poor fellows without their annual dinner.[10]

This comparison of public office to a public feast, of which all should be eligible to partake, is an image which would naturally suggest itself to a materialist like Smith and which was realistic in an age of sinecures and jobbery. In another place, Smith compiles a long list of public offices from which Catholics are excluded, from Lord Chancellor to patron of a church-living, and concludes, "Now if this is not picking the plums out of the pudding, and leaving the mere batter to the Catholics, I know not what is." [11]

Insofar as a political pamphlet is assumed to be directed to those who disagree with the writer in an attempt to win them over by logical argument, the *Peter Plymley Letters* enjoyed little if any success, despite its extraordinary popularity. An appeal to the nation's fear of Napoleon was more likely to hinder than to help the cause of Catholic emancipation, since anti-Jacobinism called forth the same kind of superpatriotism and adherence to church and king as lay behind the restrictive laws against Catholics. And, of course, the battle over Catholic emancipation went on for fourteen years after Waterloo, when fear of Napoleon had nothing to do with the issue. However, where Smith's logic failed, his wit succeeded. The *Peter Plymley Letters* helped keep the question of Catholic emancipation alive for many years, giving the Whigs an issue to rally around and encouraging supporters of toleration to join in a general denunciation of the stupidity, bigotry, and hypocrisy that Smith had ridiculed. He could not win over the opposition, but he helped unify the liberals; and, in the final analysis, such is the major purpose of political polemic.

Smith's intention to satirize, rather than win over, anti-Catholics is shown in the creation of Brother Abraham, the simple country parson to whom the letters are addressed. Though Abraham Plymley is never heard from in the course of the pamphlet, his arguments and mode of thinking are implicit in Peter's answers and refutations. The first letter starts, "Dear Abraham, A worthier and better man than yourself does not exist; but I have always told you, from the time of our boyhood, that you were a bit of a goose." [12] In contrast to Peter, the urbane, witty, sophisticated cosmopolite, with facts and figures about Ireland at his fingertips and the entire history of the church at his recall, Abraham emerges as a good, sincere, but rather stupid individual, cut off from the real issues of the day in his backward parish, too buried in reverence for the past to be aware of the present, eager to believe whatever those in power tell him, and rationalizing his religious prejudices with the conviction that he is engaged in a holy struggle with the forces of Satan.

It seems clear that Smith considered the bulk of the clergy and the squirearchy who opposed Catholic emancipation to be very like Brother Abraham. Twenty years later, in the last days of his struggle for religious toleration, he concluded an *Edinburgh Review* article with addresses "to the different opponents of the Catholic question." The first, and largest, category is the "No-Popery Fool," to whom he says, "You are made use of by men who laugh at you, and despise you for your folly and ignorance; and who, the moment it suits their purpose, will consent to emancipation of the Catholics, and leave you to roar and bellow No Popery! to Vacancy and the Moon." [13]

III   *From Catholics to Methodists*

Sydney Smith was more closely associated with the Catholic issue than with any other. After the *Peter Plymley Letters,* he continued arguing anonymously, in the *Edinburgh Review,* and publicly, in the pulpit, for religious toleration. In 1808, Smith reviewed Henry Parnell's history of the laws by which England had robbed, restricted, and degraded the Irish Catholics. A year later, he dismissed the question of a crown veto on the appointment of Catholic bishops, which seemed a major stumbling block in the way of emancipation, as a matter of little practical moment. In 1812, he praised the Duke of Sussex for a speech made before the House of Lords to plead for justice for the Catholics. In 1813, he attacked the Bishop of Lincoln, who had claimed that the laws keeping Catholics out of public office were not religious persecution and who was convinced that admission of Catholics into Parliament would destroy the Anglican establishment. When Napoleon was no longer a threat, Smith turned all of his attention to a plea for common justice. An article on the tribulations of Ireland, in 1820, pointed out the economic hardships which had resulted from religious inequality—the Irish Catholic peasant being forced to support, through direct tithes, an established church which he did not attend; and the Irish Catholic landlord leaving his native country to live in England where his wealth could purchase him a better social life than his religion allowed him to enjoy at home. Thomas Moore's *Memoirs of Captain Rock,* in 1821, gave Smith an opportunity to treat once more the long history of English persecution of Ireland. And in 1827, when a new coalition government again introduced measures in favor of the Catholics, Smith once more went over his arguments in a plea for an act of justice which would strengthen a disunified kingdom, and he again exposed the political selfishness and demagoguery which had so long deprived the Catholics of their rights.[14]

At two separate meetings of the Yorkshire clergy in 1825, called to support the government in continuing the laws against Catholics, Smith spoke for emancipation. He remained in a minority of one at one meeting and procured only two signatures on a minority petition at the other. In 1828, when the question of Catholic emancipation was before Parliament, and when a general election would refer the question to the people, Smith published *A Letter to the Electors on the Catholic Question,* repeating all of the arguments he had used in the past. And on November 5 of that same year, he preached a sermon on toleration at the Cathedral of Bristol, to which he had just been appointed Prebendary.[15]

In the spring of 1829, when two Tory leaders, the Duke of Wellington and Robert Peel, resigned themselves to the inevitable and were converted to the liberal cause of religious toleration, the restrictive laws against Catholics were finally repealed. But the established Protestant Church of Ireland remained, for many years, a source of religious and political controversy. At the time of his death, Smith was at work upon a pamphlet pleading for the establishment of the Catholic clergy in Ireland, so that the tithes and taxes paid by the Irish for the support of a church would go to the church attended by the vast majority.[16] The question of the Irish establishment was to plague the Whigs for the rest of the century and occasion frequent fallings-out between the old Whigs and their uneasy allies, the Radicals, starting with the fall of the Grey cabinet in 1835, and ending with the division of the Liberals over Home Rule and disestablishment under Gladstone in 1886.

Throughout his career as a fighter for religious equality, Sydney Smith never showed sympathy for Catholic theology, liturgy, or opinion. What he set as his goal was toleration, not brotherhood. When Daniel O'Connell, the Irish Catholic agitator, once introduced Smith to a group of Catholics as "the ancient and amusing defender of our faith," Smith laughingly interrupted and said, "Of your *cause,* if you please; *not* of your faith." [17] Even the *Peter Plymley Letters* are peppered with expressions like "the nonsense of the Roman Catholic religion," "the relic-covered jacket of a Catholic," "the thumbs and offals of departed saints," "the enormous wax candles, and superstitious mummeries, and painted jackets of the Catholic priests," and "the sanctified contents of a pump." But the prejudices which made it impossible for Smith to understand the forms and functions of religions other than his own never blinded him to the right of their adherents to worship as they pleased without political interference or civil discrimination. And, by the same token, his conviction of the injustice of religious tests for office never kept him from speaking against what he saw as the errors of dissenting religious practice.

At the same time that Sydney Smith was writing the last section of the *Peter Plymley Letters*, he was at work on the first of a series of articles for the *Edinburgh Review* attacking the religious practices and beliefs of the Methodists. The evangelical movement, which John Wesley had started within the Church of England in the middle of the eighteenth century, had, by the turn of the nineteenth, spread widely among the lower classes and had strongly influenced the beliefs and practices of almost all dissenting sects, with the exception of the Unitarians. Wesley's emphasis on spiritual conversion, making each man's personal revelation of the love of God his guide for Christian living and placing complete dependence for moral judgment upon emotional reaction rather than intellectual understanding, had led to an almost exclusive attention, in preaching, to the doctrine of personal salvation.

In addition to the objections which, as an orthodox Anglican, Smith had to a theology of enthusiasm, his own strongly moralistic approach to the purpose of religious teaching made him increasingly suspicious of the effects of evangelistic practice upon public morals. Contempt for the various evangelistic sects within and without the Church of England, all of which he lumped together under the name of Methodists, frequently crept into his writings. Allusions to William Wilberforce, the Clapham sect, Dr. Rees, and other "enthusiasts" are frequent in his reviews and in the *Peter Plymley Letters*.

Smith's first overt attack on Methodism appeared in the *Edinburgh Review* in January, 1808. In a review of *Causes of the increase of Methodism and Dissension* by Robert Acklem Ingram, Smith first protests against that writer's proposals to curb the spread of dissent by extension of the Test and Corporation Acts and other legislative and civil restrictions. The motives that prompted his defense of the Catholics operated just as strongly in favor of dissenters. Putting his faith in common sense rather than in tyrannical persecution, Smith intends to:

set before the eyes of the reader, a complete section of the tabernacle; and to present him with a near view of those sectaries, who are at present at work upon the destruction of the orthodox churches, . . . We shall use the general term of Methodism, to designate these three classes of fanatics [Arminian, Calvinist, and Anglican Evangelicals], not troubling ourselves to point out the finer shades and nicer discriminations of lunacy, but treating them all as in one general conspiracy against common sense, and rational orthodox Christianity.[18]

With an attitude half serious and half comic, Smith then proposes that a real understanding of a religious sect cannot be based merely on a knowledge of its articles of faith, but must arise from an examination of the emphasis and interpretation put upon those articles in practice. In a series of quotations from evangelical and Methodist magazines, taken out of context and given frequently ludicrous captions, he caricatures the daily practice and preaching of the "enthusiasts." Major weaknesses of the early evangelicals were their numerous unlearned clergy, a limited and somber view of election, overemotionalism in preaching and worship, and overuse of peculiar jargon. None of these was essential to the central principle of personal conversion through personal experience of divine love, on the model of St. Paul, but these were the characteristics of which Smith's method of ridicule made the most. The Methodists' designation of themselves as "Christians" and all others as "carnal people"; their condemnation of all amusements; their use of religious language in the most common and, therefore, most ludicrous contexts; their lower-class artisans-turned-preachers; and their belief in the everyday occurrence of miracles and visions are all held up to scorn by the simple means of being presented to the reader in a number of quotations, all of which, because of their use of a patent and peculiar phraseology, sound the same.

Smith defended himself against Francis Jeffrey's objection to his use of levity in attacking a religious issue. "I do not understand what you can mean by levity of quotation," he wrote. "I attack these men because they have foolish notions of religion. The more absurd the passage, the more necessary it should be displayed—the more urgent the reason for making the attack at all." [19] But Smith did not attack the Methodists merely because they were foolish. The ease with which the evangelical sects had

moved into the overcrowded urban working-class districts where
the Church of England had been slow to act seemed, to him, to
pose a greater threat to the establishment than anything the Catholics might do. He himself had tried, in 1806, to lease a chapel in
St. James parish which up to then had been occupied by a sect
calling themselves the Christians of the New Jerusalem. The Rector of St. James, Dr. Gerard Andrewes, however, had been unwilling to allow Smith to preach within his parish; and Smith's
arguing that Anglican worship should be preferred to dissent,
that he was willing to be bound by any conditions, that Dr.
Andrewes' own church was overcrowded, and that he sorely
needed the employment had been useless.[20] This experience is
reflected in the attack on Methodism, where Smith says,

As the law now stands, any man who dissents from the established
church may open a place of worship where he pleases. No orthodox
clergyman may do so, without the consent of the parson of the parish,
—who always refuses, because he does not choose to have his monopoly disturbed; and refuses, in parishes where there are not accommoda-
tions for one half of the persons who wish to frequent the Church of
England, and in instances where he knows that the chapels from which
he excludes the established worship will be immediately occupied by
sectaries.

More importantly, Smith considered the tendency of evangelicalism to make men dependent on an ultra-personal understanding
of God for moral guidance destructive of the basic purpose of
religion, which was the teaching of rational morality.

When an human being believes that his internal feelings are the monitions of God, and that these monitions must govern his conduct; and
when a great stress is purposely laid upon these inward feelings in all
the discources from the pulpit; it is, of course, impossible to say to
what a pitch of extravagance mankind may not be carried, under the
influence of such dangerous doctrines. . . .
     The Methodists lay very little stress upon practical righteousness.
They do not say to their people, Do not be deceitful; do not be idle;
get rid of your bad passions; or at least (if they do say these things)
they say them very seldom. Not that they preach faith without works;
for if they told people, they might rob and murder with impunity, the
civil magistrate must be compelled to interfere with such doctrine:
—but they say a great deal about faith, and very little about works.

This first attack on the Methodists was followed, in the next number of the *Edinburgh*, by an article on missions in India.[21] Various evangelical sects, particularly the Baptists, through influence in the East India Company, had gained great support from government officials for their missionary activities in the East. Using the same method as he had in the previous article, quoting numerous selections from the journals of the evangelicals themselves, Smith pointed out that zeal for the conversion of the Indians to Christianity was resulting in a situation not only futile but also dangerous to the interests of religion and government alike. Official support of the missionaries gave rebellious native leaders, both Hindu and Moslem, an excuse to stir up insurrections against the British Raj under the guise of religious warfare. And whatever few converts the Baptists managed to make, displaying as they did the most foolish kind of Christianity, were turned not to Christianity but away from Hinduism. The immediate loss of caste and violent persecution that Indian converts underwent at the hands of their countrymen made backsliding frequent and reacceptance as a Hindu almost impossible, so that the poor Indian was left with no religion at all. The only way to Christianize India, Smith insisted, was first to stabilize the government by avoiding any possible causes of religious uprisings. Then, in time, gradual and rational conversion might be able to take place; but the Hindus, with a greater civilization and more advanced religion than almost any other non-Christian people, were not in such great need of conversion that an empire should be risked on the slim chance of making them Christian.

Evangelical writers were ready to answer these attacks, particularly because the author, readily identified as a clergyman, relied on humor for his effects and so could be accused of trifling with sacred subjects. When Smith published his own sermons in 1809, the evangelical *Christian Observer* accused him of preaching to amuse on the seventh day as playhouses did on the other six, patronizing "vice and immorality at home," and opposing "every attempt, as yet projected, to disseminate his own religion abroad." [22] A pamphlet by John Styles, criticizing the articles on Methodists and missions, was the subject of another review by Smith in the *Edinburgh Review* for April, 1809.[23]

Here Smith repeats most of the objections to Methodism at

home and abroad which he had voiced previously, but, rather than relying on quotations for his effects, he deals more directly with both Mr. Styles's arguments and Mr. Styles himself. Smith defends his use of ridicule to attack the ridiculous; he decries the tendency of evangelical thinkers to brand as atheistic anyone who does not agree with them; he claims that he is not contemptuous of Methodists because they are poor and ignorant, but because they assume the responsibility of the powerful and learned in establishing and teaching religion; and he insists that the Methodists view the world as if they could count on the immediate help of God in all their projects and as if their missionaries were to be equated with the Apostles. Styles himself he characterizes as "the sacred and silly gentleman before us," "this bad writer," "this fanatical writer," "illiterate and ungrammatical," "our sour devotee," and even one of "those who are little curious about truth or falsehood."

But neither his contempt for the evangelicals nor his rather rough treatment by the evangelical press changed Smith's basically tolerant view of the church establishment. His first article against Methodists began with a plea for civil equality for all dissenters. Long after his attacks on the tabernacle and its Indian missionaries, he continued to write against religious persecution. In 1811, he reviewed and supported two dissenters' pleas for civil equality;[24] and in 1821, he defended and laughed at dissenters at the same time, in an article arguing that dissenters ought to be allowed to marry according to their own beliefs. "Cupid cares not for creeds; the same passion which fills the parsonage house with chubby children, beats in the breast of the Baptist,—animates the Arminian,—melts the Unitarian maid,—and stirs up the moody Methodist to declare himself the victim of human love."[25]

CHAPTER 4

Most Enlightened Understandings

I *The Scottish Philosophy*

THE most significant stage in Sydney Smith's education came some years after he left Oxford. Toward the end of 1797, he was asked by his old friend and patron, Michael Hicks Beach, to be tutor and companion to Michael, Jr., who the squire wanted to study abroad for a while before attending one of the universities. Smith's first suggestion was Germany, but Napoleon's successful campaigns against Switzerland and Italy seemed to be pointing toward French conquest of the German states, and sometime in the spring of 1798 it was decided that Smith and young Michael would take up residence in Edinburgh. The Scottish capital, the "Athens of the North," was at that time at its height as an intellectual center. Many Whig nobles, unable to send their sons on the Grand Tour because of the war, preferred that the future lords study at the University of Edinburgh where a more liberal political atmosphere existed than at Oxford or Cambridge. The great man at the University was Dugald Stewart, Professor of Moral Philosophy; other leading lights were John Playfair, the mathematician, Alexander Fraser Tytler, the historian, and Adam Walker, the natural scientist. In addition, Stewart and others were carrying on the legacy of Adam Smith in teaching the new science of political economy.

A few months after his arrival, Smith wrote to a friend, "I like this place extremely & cannot help thinking that for a literary man, by which term I mean a man that is fond of Letters, it is the most eligible situation in the Island. It unites good Libraries liberally manag'd, learned men without any other system than that of pursuing truth. . . ."[1] Smith's admiration for Edinburgh never changed, and it was with many regrets that he left the city in August, 1803, to find professional advancement in London. Years later he lamented, "When shall I see Scotland again? Never shall I forget the happy days I passed there amidst odious smells, barbarous sounds, bad suppers, excellent hearts, and most enlightened understandings." [2]

The enlightenment which Smith so admired was the product of a century of British thought. Beginning with Locke, British philosophers had tried to construct a science of human behavior and knowledge which would be as precise and empirically accurate as Newtonian physics. Locke laid the basis for such a social science by stipulating that human experience, if analyzed into individual perceptions, could yield data which, in turn, could support an inductive system of universal laws of thought and knowledge. Early in the eighteenth century, Bishop Berkeley, taking vision as his principal example, demonstrated that human knowledge was restricted to perception and that the universe existed, for man, only in being perceived. This left ultimate existence out of the realm of human experience and in the mind of God. Human perception being fallible and temporary, it could not give reality to the material universe. Only Divine perception endowed the spiritual universe with ultimate reality.

A generation after Berkeley, two men made his perceptual theory of knowledge even more inclusive and scientific. David Hume applied the Newtonian method rigidly to the area of moral philosophy and discovered that there was no knowledge apart from perception and the connections among perceptions which men formed through mere habit. This left no room for any ultimate knowledge. Hume started out to refute mechanistic theories of knowledge and concluded in opening the door to general scepticism. David Hartley, in an attempt to justify religious optimism in a mechanical universe, formulated the principle of association, which stated that knowledge consisted of associations made among perceptions to form ideas, or meaningful groups of perceptions. In his theory of vibrations, Hartley postulated a physiological as well as a psychological foundation for association.

The horror which orthodox Scotland had of Hume's implicit scepticism cast a shadow on the whole attempt to construct a scientific moral philosophy until another Scot, Thomas Reid, refuted both Hume's scepticism and Berkeley's idealism. Reid introduced "common sense," or the historically ratified general intuitive knowledge of mankind, as a valid source of truth. This left knowledge of God and faith in the reality of the universe secure while knowledge of the material world could still be examined scientifically on the basis of perceptual data. The Scottish, or "common sense," school of philosophy was centered by the end of the century in Edinburgh, where Reid's disciple, Dugald Stewart, lectured at the University.

At about the same time, Hartley's philosophy was having a revival in England. In 1775, Joseph Priestley republished Hartley's *Theory of the Human Mind*, editing out the sections on physiology and leaving only a system built on the theory of association. Thus, by the turn of the nineteenth century, there were, generally speaking, two schools of British moral philosophy—the Scottish intuitive school and the English associationist school—both based on the assumption that universal laws of human knowledge and behavior could be ascertained by the scientific method.

Dugald Stewart's most brilliant student and ultimate successor was Thomas Brown, who refuted much of Reid's "common sense" and brought Scottish philosophy closer to Hume and Hartley, oddly enough, by giving it a more metaphysical turn. Brown first gained recognition when he was only in his twenties by his refutation of Hartley's physiological theories as expanded by Erasmus Darwin in *Zoonomia* (1794). Later, by taking associationism only as a means of explaining a psychological phenomenon but leaving the underlying power of association to intuition, Brown was able to avoid the denial of causality and the scepticism implicit in Hume's statement that events and impressions are connected only by mere habit; at the same time, Brown went far beyond Reid and Stewart in utilizing the principle of associationism.

II *The Royal Institution Lectures*

During his residence in Edinburgh, Sydney Smith was fully exposed to the mainstream of Scottish philosophy. He attended the lectures of Stewart, as did the entire circle of *Edinburgh Review* acquaintances. He joined a number of associations formed for discussing moral, economic, and scientific philosophy. Stewart and his students, notably Brown, were among Smith's close personal friends. When Smith went to London, he was well acquainted with the Scottish school of thought.

In 1804, Smith was asked to deliver a series of lectures on moral philosophy at the Royal Institution, which had been founded in 1799 by a number of scientists to promote research and teaching in the sciences. In later years, its libraries and laboratories afforded many scholars the opportunities for advanced studies, but in its first decade its major function seemed to be providing popular lectures on scientific subjects to a dilletantish audience. During the early years of the nineteenth century, the lecture became a popular form of sophisticated amusement, possibly because of the general decline of the theater. Sir James Mackintosh lectured on law at Lincoln's Inn and John Flaxman on art at the Royal Academy. Smith's lectures on moral philosophy made the greatest social sensation of the period at any lectern. Neither Sir Humphrey Davy's lectures on chemistry at the Royal Institution before Smith's lectures were given, nor Coleridge's on poetry in 1808 and on Milton and Shakespeare in 1811 attracted such audiences.

Smith's first series, starting in November, 1804, drew such large crowds that the Royal Institution had to build galleries for additional seating. He was asked to deliver a second series of lectures early in 1805 and a third early in 1806. Neither Smith nor his friends took his role as philosopher very seriously. Francis Horner wrote to an Edinburgh friend, just before the first series:

I suppose you know that Smith begins to lecture on Moral Philosophy next Saturday at the Royal Institution. You would be amused to hear the account he gives of his own qualifications for the task, and his mode of manufacturing philosophy; he will do the thing very cleverly, I have little doubt, as to the general manner, and he is sufficiently aware of all the forbearances to be observed. Profound lectures on metaphysics would be unsuitable to the place; he may do some good, if he makes the subject amusing.[3]

Many years later, Smith himself wrote to Dr. William Whewell, Professor of Moral Philosophy at Cambridge:

My lectures are gone to the dogs, and utterly forgotten. I know nothing of moral philosophy, but I was thoroughly aware that I wanted £200 to furnish my house. The success, however, was prodigious; all Albemarle-street blocked up with carriages, and such an uproar as I never remember to have been excited by any other literary imposture. Every week I had a new theory about conception and perception; and supported by a natural manner, a torrent of words, and an impudence scarcely credible in this prudent age.[4]

He consigned the lectures to the fire, but they were literally snatched from the flames by his wife, who published them after his death as *Elementary Sketches of Moral Philosophy*. The book was for a time a popular introduction to psychology—it was among Dickens' favorites—but its usefulness was limited by the original purpose of the lectures, to provide an amusing and understandable account of a science that was usually deemed both profound and dull. Smith considered popularization a major purpose of the Royal Institution and its founders. In concluding his second series of lectures, he noted that he and the Institution had been adversely criticized for encouraging smatterers rather than scholars; but he defended the popularizing of material for the sake of broadening its appeal by pointing out that serious scholarship must always start with elementary knowledge and that more eggs produced more chickens.[5]

In his first lecture he makes it clear that he is not proposing anything new or original, but is teaching the thought of Berkeley, Hartley, Francis Hutcheson, Adam Smith, Hume, Reid, and Stewart on a science which, "comprehends all the intellectual, active, and moral faculties of man; the laws by which they are governed; the limits by which they are controlled; and the means by which they may be improved: it aims at discovering, by the accurate analysis of his spiritual part, the system of action most agreeable to the intentions of his Maker, and the most conducive to the happiness of man." [6]

His task as a lecturer is one mainly of definition, Smith says, since the words used in describing and analyzing human thought and emotion are in common use, and this makes precise and scientific terminology difficult. Yet, despite this warning, Smith himself often borrows the connotations and idiomatic usages of words in order to make a deductive point. For example, he argues that taste is a function of esthetic rather than moral judgment because, "It seems to have been intended that the metaphor [of taste] should apply to feelings connected with pleasure and pain, not with duties and crimes." [7] And he limits beauty to the effect on only certain senses, because the word "beautiful," "is applied to the simplest sensations of sight, as colour, figure and so forth; it is applied to sounds, either simple or compound; but, I believe, neither to touch, taste, nor smell. We should not say that the feeling of velvet, or the taste of sugar, or the smell of a rose, was beautiful: the latter instance, however, is rather doubtful; if the expression be not already legitimated, I think we may say it will be so very soon." [8] So, although he claims that the science of moral philosophy as he is teaching it is the result of a triumphant application of Baconian methods to the questions of the human mind and spirit, his lectures are far less scientific than he cares to admit.

Smith's greatest contribution to moral philosophy, as Horner predicted, is in the witty analogies and examples with which he amuses and instructs his audience. In discussing human aptitudes, he invents a metaphor which has since become a cliché through frequent use. "If you choose to represent the various parts in life by holes upon a table, of different shapes—some circular, some triangular, some square, some oblong,—and the persons acting these parts by bits of wood of similar shape, we shall find that the triangular person has got into the square hole, the oblong person into the triangular, and a square person has squeezed himself into the round hole." [9]

In arguing that human civilization is due in large part to men's ability to cooperate as well as to the superiority of human intellect, Smith says, "A lion lies under a hole in a rock; and if any other lion happen to pass by, they fight. Now, whoever gets a habit of lying under a hole in a rock, and fighting with every gentleman who passes near him, cannot possibly make any progress." [10]

The lectures are full of simple, concrete illustrations of the various theories put forth. The effect of experience on apparent perception is explained by the example of the landsman who sees only a brown lump on the horizon while the sailor sees a man-of-war; their eyes receive exactly the same image, but the association in the mind of the sailor makes the difference. Smith distinguishes among wonder, admiration, and surprise by saying, "The first time I see St. Paul's, I wonder at it; the hundredth time, I only admire it. If I wake in a coach, and find myself in St. Paul's Churchyard, when I thought I was in Pall Mall, I am surprised by the appearance of the building." [11]

III *Standpoint and Viewpoint*

The subject matter of moral philosophy is divided by Smith into three rough categories. The first series of lectures deals with the understanding; he takes up perception, conception, memory, imagination, and reason and judgment. The second series is on taste, with lectures on wit and humor, the beautiful, and the sublime; and the third concerns what he calls the active powers of the mind: the affections, the passions, and the desires. In addition, each series concludes with some sound moral advice; each of the first two series ends with a lecture "On the Conduct of the Understanding," and the third with two lectures "On Habit."

The first series shows how closely Smith adheres to the Scottish school, especially the "common sense" philosophy as expounded by Thomas Brown, who had been a weekly dinner guest of the Smiths in Edinburgh. Smith dismisses Berkeley's idealistic destruction of the material world by appealing to the inherent knowledge of mankind, and he refutes the charge of scepticism by saying that moral philosophy, like any study which aims at understanding creation, can only lead to faith in God. In both of these he expresses the orthodox Scottish point of view as Reid had founded it. But he lays far greater stress on association, as Brown and the English school found it in Hartley and Hume, than Reid and Stewart did. Not only does he ascribe all perceptual knowledge to association when, in the first series, he defends Locke, Berkeley, Hartley, and Priestley for their theories of perception (though he ridicules their physiological arguments); but, in the third series, he specifically departs from the theories of Reid and Stewart concerning the active powers of the mind. Whereas the "common sense" school categorized these powers according to their inherent causes (appetites from the body, desires from experience) or effects (affections communicate joy or pain to others, self-love aggrandizes the individual), Smith sets out to trace all the passions and affections to association. Fear, he claims, is learned from pain, ridiculing the argument that it stems from an innate terror of falling by pointing out how many other, more violent, fears the child learns. He traces grief and pain, as well as love and pleasure, to association with particular experiences; a child brought up by parents who smiled when angry and frowned when happy, he argues, would express his own emotions in the same way.

The second series is of particular interest since his lectures on wit and humor and on esthetic judgments cast light on his own writings. He defines wit as the "discovery of those relations in ideas which are calculated to excite surprise," [12] but he specifically excludes from his definition anything which is not only surprising but also beautiful, sublime, or a useful truth. He considers punning an inferior form of wit, wherein the effect lies in discovering a relationship between different sounds rather than ideas. Such a rigidly narrow definition would seem to challenge his own claim to wit; for, in his writings at least, his power of pointing up "relations in ideas which are calculated to excite surprise" is almost always used to make some point, often contentious. For example, would the following extract from the *Peter Plymley Letters* be described as wit, or as useful truth?—"You may not be aware of it yourself, most reverend Abraham, but you deny their freedom to the Catholics upon the same principle that Sarah your wife refuses to give the receipt for a ham or gooseberry dumpling; she values her receipts, not because they secure to her a certain flavour, but because they remind her that her neighbors want it." [13]

When Smith comes to define humor, he calls it "incongruity which creates surprise, and *only* surprise," laughter being brought on by a feeling of superiority in the individual who observes his own or another's "ridiculous inferiority" arising from "incongruity, or the conjunction of objects and circumstances not usually combined,—and the conjunction of which is either useless, or . . . troublesome, and not to be desired." He distinguishes between wit and humor by pointing out, "In a piece of wit there is but a single flash of surprise and pleasure; in a piece of humour, as in Don Quixote's battle with the mills, one impression follows quickly upon another, the mind is thrown into an attitude of pleasing surprise by the first occurrence of the idea, and then all the other touches of humour act one on another with a compound force and accumulated impression, till at last the convulsion of laughter ensues." [14]

By this definition, a good amount of Smith's work can be considered humor, despite its didactic purpose. For example, in considering his famous description of the pathetic resistance of the House of Lords to the great Reform Bill of 1832, the account of eye-witnesses that he suited his actions to his words by trundling an imaginary mop back and forth during his speech reinforces the notion that he was aiming at emphasizing incongruity.

I do not mean to be disrespectful, but the attempt of the Lords to stop the progress of reform, reminds me very forcibly of the great storm of Sidmouth, and of the conduct of the excellent Mrs. Partington on that occasion. In the winter of 1824, there set in a great flood upon that town—the tide rose to an incredible height—the waves rushed in upon the houses, and every thing was threatened with destruction. In the midst of this sublime and terrible storm, Dame Partington, who lived upon the beach, was seen at the door of her house with mop and pattens, trundling her mop, squeezing out the sea-water, and vigorously pushing away the Atlantic Ocean. The Atlantic was roused. Mrs. Partington's spirit was up; but I need not tell you that the contest was unequal. The Atlantic Ocean beat Mrs. Partington. She was excellent at a slop, or a puddle, but she should not have meddled with a tempest.[15]

Certain observations Smith makes on both wit and humor show why his sermons are often clever but never funny. Wit, he comments, is incompatible with sublimity. He cites a line on the miracle at the wedding in Cana, "The modest water saw its God, and blush'd," as an example of sublime intent undermined by witty execution. And he set limits on the incongruities and inferiorities at which men are willing to laugh, saying that mankind would have nothing but indignation and contempt for "the light fool who comes with the feather of wit to crumble the bulwarks of truth, and to beat down the Temples of God!" [16]

His lectures on taste, beauty, and sublimity exhibit some of the bases of his critical judgment. Artistry of any kind, he argues, depends for its success on the associations which it calls forth in its audience far more than on its intrinsic form. The beauty of green fields after a rain is intensified by the ideas of plentifulness, freshness, liberty, boundless range, innocent enjoyment, and so forth. The beauty of spherical form is apparent in a smooth globe of glass but becomes grotesque when a tree is artificially restrained or injured to cause the same shape, and a face, swollen to roundness by disease, has associations of actual pain.

In applying this principle to any work of art, Smith says, one must distinguish between the wonderful, which calls forth admiration for the artist's skill, and the beautiful, which evokes a direct emotional response through association.

See the effects of a long piece of music at a public concert. The orchestra are breathless with attention, jumping into major and minor keys, executing figures, and fiddling with the most ecstatic precision. In the midst of all this wonderful science, the audience are gaping, lolling, talking, staring about, and half devoured with ennui. On a sudden there springs up a lively little air, expressive of some natural feeling, though in point of science not worth a halfpenny: the audience all spring up, every head nods, every foot beats time, and every heart also.[17]

This is an echo of the eternal "I don't know art, but I know what I like," calling what one likes "beautiful" and what one does not know "wonderful." It does explain, if Smith is to be taken at his word, why he was never an enthusiast of music or painting. On one occasion, showing off a collection of pictures he had bought at an auction because they were cheap, he told a visitor, "But look at that sea-piece, now; what would you desire more? It is true, the moon in the corner was rather dingy when I first bought it; so I had a new moon put in for half-a-crown, and now I consider it perfect." [18]

After a Handel concert in York Minster, he wrote, "Nothing can be more disgusting than an Oratorio. How absurd to see 500 people fiddling like madmen about the Israelites in the Red Sea"; and he once declined an invitation to the opera, saying, "I love music very little,—I hate acting; . . . Moreover, it would be rather out of etiquette for a Canon of St. Paul's to go to an opera; and where etiquette prevents me from doing things disagreeable to myself, I am a perfect martinet." [19]

As for poetry, Smith ascribes its beauty to a faithful reproduction of things that are beautiful in themselves, whether natural objects, noble actions, or agreeable emotions. Measure, rhyme, and other techniques of prosody have the same effect as wit and produce admiration for the wonderful rather than appreciation for the beautiful. When poetry describes ugliness or misery, the reader can experience a kind of pleasure in contemplating, without experiencing, evil; and when it describes power, magnitude, solitude, or infinity, it can be sublime by exciting a feeling akin to terror. But in neither case is there beauty, which can come only from representation of the beauties of nature or of human goodness. Creative imagination does not endow the work with beauty, but merely consists of the ability to see all possibilities and the judgment to choose that which has the most beautiful associations. Such a view of the imagination, in Coleridgean or Wordsworthian terms, reduces it to fancy. It is no wonder, therefore, that Smith's esthetic judgments, whenever he makes any in the *Edinburgh Review,* are always based on mimetic or didactic canons.

Smith's moral philosophy, like his religious philosophy, allowed him to make a neat distinction between matters of the spirit and matters of the world. Ultimate causes were in the realm of metaphysical speculation and were to be taken on faith. However, within this spiritual framework, he could recognize that the sphere of human thought and behavior was a field for scientific investigation, capable of analysis and generalization by a few simple laws, such as association, self-interest, and the golden rule, because of man's nature being fundamentally uniform and universal. Like his sermons, his lectures are pointed toward an understanding of human behavior in order to enable his hearers to construct an ethic based on recognition and satisfaction of their own best interests. The didactic lectures with which he concludes each series are filled with good advice, directed particularly at the young. Work hard at studies, for genius is dependent on labor. Have enough curiosity to follow an interest deeply, but be able to vary your pursuits at any time. Depend on understanding for knowledge, and not on note-scribbling, "which leaves a man's wit and talents neatly written out in his common-place book, and safely locked up in the bottom drawer of his bureau." Contradict less, and listen more. Use the force of habit to become virtuous and wise. To Sydney Smith, the duties of a teacher were inseparable from those of a preacher, and he performed both.

IV *Philosophy and Politics*

The point at which moral philosophy becomes political philosophy is in the analysis of the active powers of the mind—the desires, affections, and passions which move men to action. Associationism, assuming that men developed emotions and inclinations through the experiences of pain and pleasure, concluded that individuals act always through self-interest. If, as social science demanded, human nature was fundamentally uniform, it could be concluded that the interests of the individual were identical with those of the vast majority and therefore those of society. This was the basis of Adam Smith's laissez faire political economy. In his third series of lectures, Sydney Smith points out, "If a messenger from heaven were on a sudden to annihilate the love of power, the love of wealth, and the love of esteem, in the human heart; in half an hour's time the streets would be as empty, and as silent, as they are in the middle of the night." [20]

This notion of the natural identity of interests which underlay political economy was not easily transferred to the area of social and legal philosophy. Liberal social theories based on the notions of a social contract or the rights of man ran counter to the scientific principle that the interests of the individual should contribute to, rather than be overruled by, the interests of society in general. On the other hand, a social philosophy based on a laissez faire principle as broad as that of political economy required some great central principle like the law of supply and demand to cancel out individual injustices and produce general felicity. William Godwin, in his *Enquiry Concerning Political Justice* (1793), argued that a principle of general benevolence governs the individual actions of men, and if mankind were left free to act as reason dictates in all circumstances, people would generally act in the best interests of society.

Godwin's views were unacceptable to associationists, who saw in the principle of general benevolence a motive force independent of the experience of the individual. Sydney Smith's very first article in the *Edinburgh Review* was a review and appreciation of a sermon by Dr. Samuel Parr refuting Godwin's contention. [21] Parr charged that postulating universal benevolence as the immediate motive to man's actions would tend to destroy the particular affections which are at the basis of the everyday duties of the individual and would make men neglectful of their families, associates, and own natural interests. Smith adds that Parr's rejection of universal benevolence as a motive to action should not be construed as a rejection of that principle as a criterion of action; that is, men must act according to their individual interests and affections but should measure their actions by the extent to which they are universally beneficial. Smith makes the same points in the next article, a review of Godwin's pamphlet replying to Parr and other critics.[22] In this pamphlet, Godwin himself says that the principle of universal benevolence is more justly a criterion than a motive.

This principle, that the individual's actions on the basis of self-interest should (rather than must) contribute to the general interest, laid the basis for the democratic social philosophies of the nineteenth century. Jeremy Bentham, even before Godwin, recognized that in the sphere of law there must be a framework of legislation to reconcile, by artificial means, the natural differences between self-interest and the general interest. Bentham's moral arithmetic of pleasure and pain and the legal systems he evolved from it all rose from the associationist moral philosophy which stated that man acted according to learned motives. It was Bentham's disciple, James Mill, who brought Bentham's utilitarianism and Hume-Hartley associationism together into what became known as Radicalism, postulating that since self-love is universal and that the purpose of government is to achieve the greatest happiness of the greatest number, democracy is the system to reconcile general interest and self-interest by following the will of the majority until the majority approaches unanimity and differences of interest disappear.

The notion that ultimate justice lay in granting absolute power to the people was very different from the principles of Whig liberalism, which assumed that all power was intrinsically evil and all people perversely selfish and that government existed in order to distribute power among various interests and groups in order to keep each from exercising unjust tyranny over the others. This led the Whigs to oppose centralized authoritarian government, whether absolute monarchy or absolute democracy, and

to seek individual solutions to particular social and political griev-
ances rather than to try to institute general reforms aimed at
simplifying the intricate checks-and-balances system of government. Since the Whigs saw themselves as representing property,
and saw property as the interest most closely akin to the general
interest of the nation, they continued to act according to their
own motives, convinced that they would be acting in the best
interests of all and that other interests, crown, church, and such,
would have means of offsetting any deviation from the general
good.

Widespread working-class agitation in 1816 and 1817 and the
resultant suppressive measures taken by the Tory Liverpool government brought Whigs and Radicals closer together in opposing
both rabble-rousers on the left and reactionaries on the right. In
1827, Lord Grey did not think that a reform of Parliament, the
major goal of the Radicals, was yet a basic principle on which to
form a Whig government, but by 1830 he took office with the
express purpose of passing a reform bill. The Whigs who worked
for this Radical program of reform did so according to their own
principles, not those of the Radicals. Seeing in the unenfranchised
middle class a powerful danger to the continued existence of established institutions, they advocated reform in order to ally the
rich and educated merchant and manufacturing classes to the
aristocracy, attempting both to broaden the base of the government's representation of property and to take from the working-
class mobs their most effective leaders in clamoring for democracy. Francis Baring's definition of Whiggery in the mid-thirties
was a little exalted in tone but accurate on the whole, "A body
of men connected with high rank and property, bound together
by hereditary feelings, party ties, as well as higher motives, who
in bad times keep alive the sacred flame of freedom, and when
the people are roused stand between the constitution and revolution and go with the people, but not to extremities." [23] For half
a century after the Reform Bill of 1832, the Whigs continued to
exercise influence far out of proportion to their numbers in the
Liberal alliance with the Radicals, tempering and guiding the
popular movements which the Radicals headed in order to put
off change for as long as possible and then to accept the inevitable
with timely concessions.

The closest Sydney Smith came to being a Radical, a proponent of reform as a general principle rather than as a specific means of relieving a specific wrong, was in 1825, when he reviewed Jeremy Bentham's *Book of Fallacies*.[24] The volume had been put together by an anonymous editor from some of Bentham's unfinished papers and published by John and Leigh Hunt in 1824. In his review, Smith took on the task of a middleman in order to reduce Bentham's length, obscurity, and occasional tediousness to presentable and understandable order, to make his readers, "acquainted with Mr. Bentham through the medium of Reviews—after that eminent philosopher has been washed, trimmed, shaved, and forced into clean linen." The essay describes the way measures are blocked in Parliament by a number of fallacious methods of argument, from calling the ignorance of the past "the wisdom of our ancestors" to confusing the measure proposed with the man who proposes it and a charge against a public office with a slur upon the officeholder. The review concludes with "Noodle's Oration," a hypothetical address combining all of the fallacies defined and exposed by Bentham.

Thus, Smith found himself fighting prejudice, fear of change, and irrational argument, the bugbears which he had opposed so often in the past. But by 1825, he also found himself, and the Whig party, closer to the Radicals than ever before, in arguing against the very spirit of reaction rather than the manifestation of that spirit in opposition to Catholic emancipation, toleration of dissenters, abolition of slavery, popular education, or some other piece of progressive legislation.

During the difficult days of 1831 and 1832, when the resistance of the House of Lords and the clergy of the Church of England to the Reform Bill led to a precarious social condition throughout England, when Tory lords were boarding up their houses against the mobs, workingmen's associations were arming and drilling in preparation for civil war, and crowds burned bishops in effigy on Guy Fawkes Day, Sydney Smith made a number of speeches supporting reform. His depiction of the Lords as old Dame Partington, fighting the sea with her mop, gave the country something to laugh at, at a time when laughter was the only relief to hatred, bitterness, and suspicion. A noted historian has said, "Such laughter was like light in a darkened landscape, bearing hope of a peaceful victory. There was no such kindly laughter heard in France in 1789." [25]

Of all the issues which followed the Reform Bill itself, the question of secret balloting was the one on which the Radicals came closest to overcoming the Whigs and which most aptly demonstrated the differences in point of view of the two groups of liberals. The Radicals, with their view of government as a means of finding expression for the self-interest of all individuals, favored the secret ballot and, eventually, universal franchise. The Whigs, still regarding political power as both a privilege and a form of property, held that the voter was an especially responsible individual, given his franchise because his property made him a fit representative of the national interest. This meant that secret voting freed the elector from the influence and observation of the unenfranchised masses whose interests he was supposed to represent. The propertied elector had a constituency just as the member of Parliament did, and should be held responsible for how he used his authority.

In 1839, Sydney Smith published a pamphlet against the ballot.[26] He offered a number of well-thought-out arguments to show that the charges of bribery, coercion, and hypocrisy under the present system were greatly exaggerated and that these evils would not be all diminished by secret voting. But central to his argument was the Whig notion of representative property. He called electors "only trustees for those who have no vote," and called for open and honest declarations of political allegiance and responsibility:

"Who brought that mischievous profligate villain into Parliament? Let us see the names of his real supporters. Who stood out against the strong and uplifted arm of power? Who discovered this excellent and hitherto unknown person? Who opposed the man whom we all know to be one of the first men in the country?" Are these fair and useful questions to be veiled hereafter in impenetrable mystery? Is this sort of publicity of no good as a restraint? Is it of no good as an incitement to and a reward for exertions? Is not public opinion formed by such feelings? and is it not a dark and demoralising system to draw this veil over human actions, to say to the mass, be base, and you will not be despised; be virtuous, and you will not be honoured?

V The Throes of Partisanship

Sydney Smith's support of the Whig philosophical position during the years of reform arose not only from his views on moral philosophy but also from the partisan stand he had taken years before in the *Edinburgh Review*. From the beginning, the *Review* had a Whiggish political coloration. Founded in the midst of a widespread reaction to the French Revolution and suspicion of any liberal sentiments, the *Edinburgh* constantly took a half-disgusted, half-amused view of rampant anti-Jacobinism. Smith exemplified this attitude in his review of a volume of sermons by Dr. Rennel, when he said:

We . . . blame him for having selected for publication so many sermons touching directly and indirectly upon the French Revolution. We confess ourselves long since wearied with this kind of discourses, bespattered with blood and brains, and ringing eternal changes upon atheism, cannibalism, and apostasy. . . . The public are disgusted with it to satiety; and we can never help remembering, that this politico-orthodox rage in the mouth of a preacher may be profitable as well as sincere.[27]

Smith had spent six months in France in 1789 and had enrolled as "Citoyen Smith, membre affilié au Club des Jacobins de Montvilliers" in Normandy, both for his own safety and out of sympathy for the revolutionary cause. Sensitive to injustice and want, he was always inclined to support the cause of an individual or a people against the force of power, privilege, or wealth. But he was too close an observer of human nature to believe in the perfectibility of man or man's institutions. From the beginnings of the French Revolution, he was aware of the dangers of sudden populism and was spared the bitter disillusionment that the Reign of Terror and the rise of Napoleon brought to many of his friends and contemporaries. In his ability to differentiate between the valuable contributions of the French Revolution to the cause of liberalism and the tragic results of its explosive energy, he avoided the worst errors of both British attitudes on France. Unlike Charles James Fox and his closest supporters, he did not feel impelled to oppose the war against Napoleon or constantly defend French excesses to the extent that earned many Whigs a reputation for treason. One could never picture him in the red cap with which political cartoonists continually adorned their caricatures of Fox and Sheridan.

In 1803, Smith reviewed *Dernières Vues de Politiques, et de Finance,* by Jacques Necker, an *émigré* who had been Minister of Finance under Louis XVI. Smith examines Necker's proposals for an ideal constitutional republic, such as France should establish, with close attention to problems of practical politics and with great distrust of revolutionary change and grandiose plans for overnight constitutions.

The miserable dilemma in which men living under bad governments are placed, is, that without a radical revolution, they may never be able to gain liberty at all; and, with it, the attainment of liberty appears to be attended with almost insuperable difficulties. . . . A nation grown free in a single day is a child born with the limbs and the vigour of a man, who would take a drawn sword for his rattle, and set the house in a blaze, that he might chuckle over the splendour.[28]

But Smith's own reservations about the French Revolution did not blind him to the harm done by the superpatriots, who urged eternal war against France until the Bourbon dynasty should be restored. When the Peace of Amiens brought a relief from the expenses and hardships of war in 1802, many Pittites were eager to renew the war immediately, rather than allow Napoleon, just elected Consul for life, to solidify his position on the Continent. John Bowles wrote a pamphlet urging renewal of war, and Smith reviewed it, saying, "The truth is, if Mr. Bowles had begun his literary career at a period when superior discrimination and profound thought, not vulgar violence and the eternal repetition of rabble-rousing words, were necessary to literary reputation, he would never have emerged from that obscurity to which he will soon return. The intemperate passions of the public, not his own talents, have given him some temporary reputation; . . ." Later, after quoting a passage of Bowles' superpatriotism, Smith comments, "We seriously commend in Mr. Bowles this future dedication to the service of his King and country; and consider it as a virtual promise that he will write no more in their defence." [29]

As time went on, the *Edinburgh Review* became even more partisan in its outlook. From reaction against anti-Jacobinism the *Review* advanced to a position of support of the more liberal Whigs, followers of C. J. Fox, who were proponents of parliamentary reform and religious toleration. In 1808, Walter Scott took the first steps in starting a review to oppose the *Edinburgh*. He had quarreled with Archibald Constable over publication of his edition of Swift's works and had taken offense at Jeffrey's review of *Marmion*. When an article appeared in the *Edinburgh* reviewing a state paper by Don Pedro Cevallos, the Spanish Secretary of State, and attacking the existence of landed aristocracy,[30] it seemed obvious that the *Edinburgh Review* had committed itself to a far more liberal position than Scott cared to associate with, and he proposed to William Gifford that they start a rival journal. They enlisted the aid of George Canning, Robert Southey, and others, and the first issue of the *Quarterly Review* was published in February, 1809.

The appearance of the *Quarterly* started a journalistic rivalry that lasted for many years. In the first issue, an article by Southey, "Account of the Baptist Missionary Society," covers the same ground as Smith's article on "Indian Missions" but argues that the Indian missions had nothing to do with any rebellions and that the case was totally misrepresented by those writers who misquoted and distorted the journals of the missionaries. The purpose of the reviewer was to attack Smith and the *Edinburgh* as well as to defend the Baptist missionaries.[31]

A review of Smith's 1809 volume of sermons, by John Wilson Croker, appeared in the second issue of the *Quarterly*. After ridiculing Smith's insistence, in an earlier volume of sermons, on the importance of gesture and appealing language to effective preaching, Croker turned to the 1809 publication and found it Socinian in doctrine, political in its insistence on toleration for the Catholics, and inconsistent with Smith's attacks on Methodism. In February, 1810, Croker again reviewed a sermon of Smith's, this time on the Catholic question, and treated his victim in the same biting style with which Smith had dispatched many authors himself.[32]

The appearance of the *Quarterly* added to the difficulties that partisanship had brought to the *Edinburgh Review*. Jeffrey's article on Don Cevallos had not only alienated Scott and other Tory subscribers and contributors but had also caused concern among staunch Whig supporters. Horner thought that the review had become far too political; he objected to the partisanship and lack of dignity in taking up quarrels with the *Quarterly* and broke off his contributions after November, 1809.

But if Horner objected to partisanship, Sydney Smith gloried in it. Secure in his church living, at ease among the aristocracy, and apparently immune to counterattacks, he was eager to take on party issues in reviews. His writings in favor of Catholic emancipation and toleration of dissenters, of course, started in this spirit. When George Rose, a Tory politician and writer, attacked the *History of the Early Part of the Reign of James II*, by Charles James Fox, as a way of attacking the memory of the author, Smith vigorously defended the late leader of his party and exposed Mr. Rose as a historical blunderer and party hack whose avowed purpose (a vindication of Sir Patrick Hume, a person supposedly maligned in Fox's history) was merely a cover for a general attack on the Whig party of 1809.[33] In the same issue of the *Edinburgh Review*, Smith reviewed and quoted from a commemorative volume, edited under a pseudonym by Dr. Samuel Parr, which collected a number of panegyrics of Mr. Fox by various persons in public life. Although Smith could not refrain from a few jokes at the expense of the pedantic Dr. Parr, his praise of Fox is unstinting.[34] And when, two years later, a work appeared attacking Rose's criticism of Fox on more scholarly grounds than those of Smith's review, Smith incorporated the material into another partisan article.[35]

A good example of the way in which partisanship affected editorial policy in the *Edinburgh Review* is the handling of the ill-fated Walcheren expedition. In July, 1809, a British expedition had been sent to the Scheldt River to destroy French shipping in and around Antwerp. The general commander of the expedition was the Earl of Chatham, an inexperienced and generally incompetent soldier; the naval commander was Sir Richard Strachan who had little use for Chatham, the army, or the whole plan of the expedition. In a campaign of almost two months, the army succeeded only in capturing the island of Walcheren, in the mouth of the river. Because of the indecision of the British commanders, the unexpected fortifications and immediate reinforcements of the French, and the large British losses to the diseases of pestilential swamps around their position, the expedition was forced to return to England in September without doing nearly as much damage to the French as to themselves. A small detachment was left behind to guard Walcheren, but, wasted by fever, it had to be withdrawn in December, nullifying the small British gains. A popular jingle went around Britain:

> Lord Chatham, with his sword undrawn,
> Kept waiting for Sir Richard Strachan;
> Sir Richard, eager to be at 'em,
> Kept waiting for the Earl of Chatham.

The real blame for failure was soon placed upon George Canning, the Foreign Secretary, and Lord Castlereagh, the War Secretary, who had planned and authorized the campaign and appointed the commanders. Immediately after the failure at Walcheren, Canning asked Castlereagh to resign. Castlereagh concluded that he was being used as a scapegoat, openly challenged Canning to a duel, and, when they met on September 21, wounded the Foreign Secretary in the thigh. In October, Canning published a *Letter to the Earl Camden,* defending his actions.

Smith immediately proposed to Jeffrey that Canning's pamphlet be reviewed in the *Edinburgh.* Spencer Perceval had taken over the ministry in the middle of October, upon the illness of the Duke of Portland, and Smith was eager to make political capital of the falling out of two Portland ministers just at the time that a new cabinet was being formed. Jeffrey, however, was reluctant to allow Smith to embroil the *Edinburgh* in partisan politics at that time, with the *Quarterly* poised to retaliate. He was ready, however, to make a defensive move if the rival journal started a political squabble. On December 22, 1809, he wrote to Lord Holland's physician and companion, John Allen, "I see the Quarterly announced, with Canning's Statement as its leading article. This is keeping clear of politics with a vengeance! Smith wrote me offering to take that subject. I rather dissuaded him, but if they make any push I think I should let him try his hand." [36] The review of Canning's pamphlet duly appeared in the *Quarterly,*

but was the sixteenth rather than the lead article of the issue.
Though the article excuses Canning of any intentional insult to
Castlereagh, it is not a strongly partisan piece of work. For one
thing, there is no mention of current cabinet formation or any
issues before the House. For another, the opening section condemns both ministers for dueling.[37]

Jeffrey, with or without the "push," took a partisan stand himself. In the next issue of the *Edinburgh Review*, he published
an article on "The State of Parties," which deals briefly with the
Canning–Castlereagh dispute. Brushing off the duel as an insignificant "squabble," Jeffrey takes up a partisan position on a larger
issue. He first pictures Britain as torn between two massive ex-
tremist parties, absolutists and democrats, with only the Whigs
in the middle to avoid catastrophe by guiding the democratic
masses from the support of anarchy to the support of constitutional and limited monarchy. This is the role in which Whiggery
pictured itself for the rest of the nineteenth century. If Parliament
votes to support the cabinet which bungled the Walcheren expedition, Jeffrey warns, a civil war may break out before the
Whigs can gain control of the indignant masses.[38]

As a matter of fact, Parliament did investigate the Walcheren
expedition and did uphold the decisions of Canning and Castlereagh; and England did not experience civil war. Smith wrote
to Jeffrey, saying, "I am sure you will excuse me for saying that
I was struck with nothing in your 'State of Parties' but its extreme
temerity, and with the incorrectness of its statements." [39] Smith
was not the only *Edinburgh* reviewer who disapproved of the
article, for Jeffrey wrote to John Allen a little later, "You all
clamor against my review of parties, and yet, does not all that
is doing in London, Westminster, and Middlesex, prove that I am
right?" [40]

When Smith finally did publish an article on the Walcheren
expedition in February, 1811, the subject was out of date. In the
first paragraph of the article he apologizes for the delay but points
out, "It is never too late to reap the dear-bought fruits of disastrous experience: and, while the men are yet alive, and moving
in the visible front of public life, who planned this lamentable
expedition, and supported it by their votes, it cannot be without
its use, to lay calmly and dispassionately before the public, one

great, finished, and elaborate specimen of the talents by which they are governed." [41] He goes on to criticize Canning and Castlereagh for sending an expedition ostensibly to the aid of Austria sixteen days after Austria had capitulated to Napoleon; deciding on a course of action against the advice of all competent military men and without accurate intelligence; appointing a proven incompetent as commander for purely political reasons; and sending a British army into a pestilential swamp in the summer without previous medical advice or adequate medical aid. The article, of course, was a year too late to have any effect on the parliamentary investigation of the campaign, but it came at a time when the Regency had just been declared and the Prince of Wales was about to choose his cabinet. The intent was as political as Jeffrey's had been a year before, and as unsuccessful. The Prince Regent kept his father's Tory cabinet in office.

A year and a half after the Walcheren article, Smith once more tackled a strictly political subject. In the spring of 1812, after the assassination of Spencer Perceval, there had been an attempt to form a coalition government.[42] First, Lord Wellesley had been empowered by the Prince to plan, but not to form, a Tory government. When neither Wellesley nor Lord Moira, a close friend of the Prince, was able to do this, the Regent empowered Wellesley to deal with the Whig leaders. In a series of letters and conferences, Wellesley offered the Whigs partial representation in the cabinet and immediate consideration of the Catholic question. When Lords Grey and Grenville refused to accept the offer, the Prince Regent resurrected his old Tory rump cabinet with Lord Liverpool as Prime Minister.

In his article, Smith blames the Whigs for being overpunctilious and demanding far too many policy concessions. Though he calls the error of the Whig leaders one on the side of generosity, he deplores their losing the opportunity to do at least something about Catholic emancipation and relations with the United States, simply because they could not do everything they wanted at once. Lord Wellesley is praised for the honor and fairness he displayed throughout the negotiations, and Lord Moira is condemned for his selfishness and duplicity.[43] What Smith overlooked in his hasty condemnation of Grey and Grenville was that the partial cabinet offered the Whigs was too small to assure the achievement of any liberal policies at all. Even the promised concession of Catholic emancipation, the issue which most interested Smith, was doubtful because of the strong anti-Catholic convictions of Lords Melville and Eldon who would also be in the government. The duplicity which he detected was not so much that of Lord Moira but that of Moira's master, the Prince Regent, who seemed to have intended to offer the Whigs just enough to appear fair but not enough to make them accept. Smith's removal from London to Yorkshire made it difficult for him to understand much of the political maneuvering barely hinted at in the official papers and correspondence published in the *Annual Register,* upon which he based his review. His isolation in Foston also explains why he did not write more strictly political articles. When dealing with personalities, Smith was a master of wit and satire; on broad partisan issues, he was incisive in getting to the philosophical or emotional core of stands and policies; but once exiled to the north, he was unable to judge the interplay of motives and methods that made up the world of everyday political activity.

CHAPTER 5

Popular Causes

I *The Bell-Lancaster Dispute*

AMONG the phenomena which new ideas brought to England during the nineteenth century, none was more important than popular education. Toward the end of the eighteenth century, the Sunday school movement provided the first opportunities for large numbers of lower-class children to receive some instruction in the rudiments of reading and writing. The Sunday School Society was founded in 1785 largely by evangelical dissenters, and the Church of England quickly followed by establishing similar weekly schools. Sydney Smith instituted such a school in Netheravon in 1794.

The first step in establishing day schools for the poor was also taken by dissenters. In 1798, Joseph Lancaster, a Quaker, established a school in the slums of London. He organized the boys themselves into a faculty of monitors who could carry on their own education with the aid of simplified lessons and various instructional devices and with a discipline based on a carefully worked out system of little rewards and punishments covering every possible offense or achievement. The whole school was supervised by one master, Lancaster, who taught a thousand children this way. Lancaster's methods, which enabled him to provide an elementary education at the annual cost of five shillings a child, were soon imitated in the United States, where there was a great deal of enthusiasm for the principle of cheap, or even free, popular education. The state of New York established its first Lancasterian school in 1805, and many others were founded in America in the next two decades.

Lancaster met with a far cooler reception at home in England. The notion of popular education seemed a dangerous one to many anti-Jacobin Englishmen, and the activities of a dissenter seemed a threat to the Church of England, which had always dominated British education through the two great universities.

Among Lancaster's critics was Mrs. Sarah Kirby Trimmer, a well-known writer of children's books who was active in the Sunday school movement. Mrs. Trimmer, suspicious of the motives and methods of a dissenter, attacked Lancaster in a pamphlet whose main arguments were religious rather than pedagogical. Francis Horner had been very favorably impressed by Lancaster's methods and principles and intended writing a review dealing severely with Mrs. Trimmer; but he had to abandon it for lack of time in December, 1805. Smith then wrote the review, which was published in the *Edinburgh* in October, 1806.[1] The purpose of the article is to refute Mrs. Trimmer rather than to defend Lancaster, and since that lady's primary objections to Lancaster's system are that it tends to replace the education of the Church of England with that of a dissenting sect and that certain of Lancaster's methods tend to irreligion, Smith's arguments are concerned with the familiar grounds of intolerance. Far from usurping the work of the Anglican church, Smith says, any teaching done by dissenting sects tends to fill the void which the establishment has left in the education of the poor. And all of Mrs. Trimmer's objections to Lancaster's Quakerism or use of precept rather than scripture to teach religious morality are dismissed as silly arguments, raised with the knowledge that an accusation of irreligion, however irrational, can arouse more concern and do more harm to a man's reputation than any reasoned evaluation of the real issues.

A year later, Smith published a second article dealing with Lancaster's school, this time not to defend the Quaker teacher from attacks but to explain his methods.[2] Smith praises Lancaster for a number of things: the combination of spelling, reading, and writing into a single lesson so that all the boys could be engaged all the time and could learn from one another; the use of slates, large lettered cards, oral instruction, and graded classes in order to make the most of whatever books and equipment were available; the creation of a miniature order of merit whereby boys who excelled could be recognized, honored, and therefore emulated; giving toys as prizes in order to encourage the students by more than a vague promise of future benefits from education; punishing those who misbehaved or failed to learn by shaming them with an emblematic sign of their offense, rather than by flogging; and establishing the whole school on such a rigid, systematic plan of instruction that monitors could take the place of masters. Above all, Smith praises Lancaster for devising a method of extending education to the lower classes, a social duty that had too long been neglected. "Nature scatters talents in a very capricious manner over the different ranks of society. It is not improbable but a general system of education would rescue some very extraordinary understandings from oblivion."

The willingness of the Quakers and other dissenters to undertake the education of the poor frightened the Church of England into establishing a broader system of mass education than weekly sermons and a few Sunday schools. In order to set up Anglican schools throughout the nation, the National Society was founded in 1811. General superintendent was Dr. Andrew Bell, who had established a school in Madras using pupil-teachers and whose work had been imitated and improved by Lancaster. Sydney Smith was very suspicious of the willingness of the Anglican Church to teach its parishioners much more than "the principles of Tithe paying, etc., etc. . . . That the Church should make itself useful, and bestir itself to diffuse Secular knowledge among the poor and continue to do so for any length of time is scarcely credible." [3] Many of Smith's friends and associates were similarly suspicious of Anglican education. Leading Whigs supported Lancaster against the intolerance of Church-and-King Tories. Brougham, Samuel Whitbread, and even the Prince of Wales (before he became Regent) were early supporters of the Lancasterian schools which were founded by the Friends and others in 1808. And when the Lancaster forces founded the British and Foreign School Society in 1814, Lords Holland, Lansdowne, and John Russell were among its patrons.

For a while, controversy between the two systems of popular education became widespread. Coleridge, scheduled to give a lecture on *Romeo and Juliet* at the London Philosophical Society, spoke instead in defense of flogging and against Lancaster's disciplinary methods of punishing by shame; in *The Friend,* he praised Bell directly and enthusiastically as the man who brought light to the ignorant masses. The Benthamites, particularly James Mill, supported Lancaster as a pioneer of universal nonsectarian education as part of their growing anticlericism. For the central issue in the dispute was a religious one. When Brougham introduced a bill for the establishment of National Parochial Schools in 1820, he was unable to satisfy either Anglicans or dissenters. A compromise measure, offering to limit weekday religious instruction to nonsectarian Bible readings and to admit non-Anglicans as teachers, frightened the Church of England by its concessions and failed to win support from dissenters, who would not accept compulsory Anglican Sunday school. It was not until 1833, when the reformed Parliament divided twenty thousand pounds between the National Society and the British and Foreign School Society, that the government, still leaving control of the schools to the churches, entered the field of popular education.

II   *Class Education and Classical Education*

Besides the religious conflict over who should teach the people, there was a conflict over what should be taught to them. Sydney Smith deplored the narrowness of British education—both in the small number of children who were taught and the limited scope of the subject matter. In his articles on Lancaster, Smith stressed the importance of extending learning to all classes as a means of strengthening the kingdom as well as benefiting the individual, and scorned the generally held impression that education would only serve to make the poor discontent with their lot. Ignorance breeds mobs, he argued, and education dispels ignorance.

With a greater part of the population being educated, there was obviously a need for a new approach to curriculum. The study of the classics could no longer be considered the final end of all schooling. First of all, the classical curriculum had been intended to train the ruling class; but the ruling class no longer had a monopoly on schooling, and had not had even before Lancaster. Secondly, the nature of society and government was rapidly changing; and even the ruling class could not depend strictly on rhetoric to govern a kingdom but needed some knowledge of the scientific and economic disciplines which had so much influence on the health of the nation.

In 1809, Smith found the opportunity to express his views on

the classical curriculum in a review of Richard Edgeworth's
Professional Education.[4] Smith takes up only one part of Edgeworth's book, its objections to the exclusive concentration on
classical learning, and makes the argument his own. He grants
that the study of the classics was of incalculable benefit in past
ages, when the wisdom of the ancients was a necessary guide
to emerging European learning; but, he states, gratitude for the
lessons of the past should not take the place of concern with the
problems of the present. Then too, the real reason for studying
the classics has been forgotten, for veneration for the wisdom of
the ancient authors has become veneration for the languages
themselves, and scholars have become completely involved in
Latin and Greek, rather than Romans and Athenians. "The picture which a young Englishman, addicted to the pursuit of knowledge, draws—his *beau idéal,* of human nature—his top and
consummation of man's powers—is a knowledge of the Greek
language. His object is not to reason, to imagine, or to invent;
but to conjugate, decline, and derive."

Smith insists that he means no disrespect to classical scholars,
nor does he intend to banish Latin and Greek from the schools.
However, there is no longer any justification for a purely classical
curriculum. Classics are excellent means to train the mind, instill
habits of study and application, and develop the powers of com-
position and oratory. But once a boy is fit to exercise his own
reason, he should study,

the mischief occasioned by bad laws, and the perplexity which arises
from numerous laws,—the causes of national wealth,—the relations of
foreign trade,—the encouragement of manufactures and agriculture,
—the fictitious wealth occasioned by paper credit,—the laws of population,—the management of poverty and mendicity,—the use and abuse
of monopoly,—the theory of taxation,—the consequences of the public
debt. These are some of the subjects, and some of the branches of civil
education to which we would turn the minds of future judges, future
senators, and future noblemen.

Smith's stand against classicism involved him in a battle with
Edward Copleston, then a Fellow of Oriel College, Oxford, and
Professor of Poetry, later, Provost of Oriel, Bishop of Llandaff,
and, as Dean of St. Paul's, Smith's colleague and superior. Coples-

ton published a pamphlet called *A Reply to the Calumnies of the Edinburgh Review against Oxford,* printed privately at Oxford in 1810. He argues in defense of the university against three articles which had appeared in the *Edinburgh:* one by John Playfair on the teaching of mathematics and Aristotelian physics, one by Richard Payne Knight on the inaccuracies in an Oxford edition of Strabo, and the one by Smith. The section which deals with Smith tries to refute him on the basis of his glib sprightliness and the inaccuracies of his allusions to trivial Greek scholarship (which Smith intended to appear nonsensical, and which, therefore, when taken seriously by Copleston, tended to prove Smith's point). Smith's reply in the *Edinburgh* is just as evasive of the real issues of the dispute.[5] He does repeat, briefly, his previous arguments against classicism, but rather than trying to build a specific case against Oxford (something even his first article did not do), he instead attacks Copleston for misquoting what he had said and for employing pedantic and overelaborate diction.

Despite his apparent regard for Oxford, Smith was not reluctant to attack traditional institutions as well as the content of British education. A few months after the Copleston review, he took up the public schools, those institutions of old endowment and large size generally thought the only proper place for the education of a gentleman, and poured on them a violent stream of criticism drawn from his own bitterly unhappy experiences at Winchester.[6] He first points to the system of fagging, upheld by a long tradition and made necessary by the large number of students, as a means for inflicting such misery on the young boys and making such conceited tyrants of the older ones that it is an evil unjustified even by the benefits claimed for public schools. And he admits of few such benefits. Athletics are of little use in later life and only discourages scholarship. The size of the schools makes adequate supervision by the masters impossible and encourages laziness in all but the most zealous scholars and debauchery in many of the weaker ones. The most impressive part of the essay is a long list of eminent men who did not attend public schools, but small private ones if any at all. Poets from Spenser to Burns, scientists from Newton to Davy, statesmen from Burleigh to Pitt, and philosophers from Bacon to Stewart —all are cited to refute the popular fallacy that "almost every conspicuous person is supposed to have been educated at public schools."

Smith proposes that the best means of education is in a private school, small enough for the master to supervise actively the studies and morals of each boy without having to appoint juvenile tyrants, and large enough for each boy to gain some insight into the variety of human character and to have both superiors to emulate and inferiors to inspire.

Some of Smith's arguments against classical education and public schools were repeated many years later in a review he wrote of a new system of teaching languages.[7] James Hamilton had published a number of literal interlinear translations, in various languages, which had met with a mixed reception. Smith praises Hamilton enthusiastically, calling a word-for-word rendering the best way to teach a language and blaming the pedants for their attachment to the form, rather than the function, of instruction in the classical tongues. Smith says that the whole obsolete apparatus of Greek lexicons with Latin definitions and complex grammar lessons without sense or use are retained by the same obstinacy that he earlier pointed to as supporting the tyrannical fagging system in public schools—the determination of each generation of parents to subject their sons to whatever hardships they went through themselves.

In another review, Smith attacked the narrowness of the education then given to women.[8] His arguments that women are capable of being taught more than sewing, painting china, and music; that educating girls would not make them unfit wives and mothers; and that society benefits from educated minds and cannot afford to neglect half the brains in the kingdom are of interest mainly in showing the prejudices that educational reform had to overcome. The notion that schools existed for the purpose of training ruling-class men in rhetoric and classical literature for use in the debates of Parliament and the conduct of affairs of state was only gradually changed to a view of education as the right and responsibility of every child in the country. Smith himself showed many traces of the old, humanistic philosophy, in arguing that new needs of government demanded changes in curriculum. His own interest in political economy and utilitarian legal philosophy led him to lay great stress on these subjects, but in his support of Lancaster and his remarks on female education he showed himself clearly in favor of universal education. His views are representative of those which governed the expansion of education during the Victorian era. Along with the eventual establishment of free, universal, elementary education and the introduction of the physical and social sciences even into Oxford and Cambridge, there was a proliferation of public schools modeled after Dr. Arnold's Rugby, offering the classical curriculum to a whole new ruling class, the wealthy trade and professional people, who were finally being admitted to the ranks of the elite and wanted for their sons the traditional education of a gentleman.

III   *The Parson and the Poachers*

During the years that Sydney Smith was publishing his essays on classical education and public schools, he was living in Heslington, hoping that a change of fortune would allow him to leave Yorkshire and return to London. However, his efforts and those of his influential friends to exchange his parish for one in the south were fruitless; and once Smith had reconciled himself to spending the rest of his career in Yorkshire, he devoted himself to making the best of his remote situation. He borrowed money to build a new rectory at Foston. He let some of his land and farmed the rest himself. He taught his children at home until the boys were old enough to go to public schools. More than anything else, he devoted his attention to the life of the agricultural poor who were his parishioners. He was, as he described himself, "village parson, village doctor, village comforter, village magistrate, and Edinburgh Reviewer." [9]

Smith's close association with the lowest classes and his responsibility for their material, as well as spiritual, welfare turned his attention to a number of social problems. It became apparent to him that the world of the poor was a very different one from that of the rich. The zeal with which he had taken up the cause of religious toleration was redirected to correct injustices against, not a religious minority, but the vast economic majority.

In 1814, Smith had stopped writing for the *Edinburgh Review,* partly because he had just moved into his rectory and farm at Foston and was busy with agricultural and parochial duties, partly because Jeffrey had taken leave from the journal that year to go to America to be married, and Smith had not gotten along well with the temporary editors. By 1818, however, the financial strain to which his building debts had subjected him convinced Smith that he should go back to his pen to supplement his income. He wrote to Jeffrey asking for forty pounds a sheet and was soon back among the reviewers at forty-five pounds.

During his four years' absence from the arena of political journalism, a significant change had occurred. With the Napoleonic wars over and the combination of disarmament, poor harvests, and technological unemployment creating extremely hard conditions among the poor, agitation for parliamentary and other reforms had brought the Whigs into a closer alliance with the Radicals. In 1816, Brougham had re-entered Parliament, after a few years' inactivity, with a program for the Whigs calling for popular education, abolition of slavery, the freedom of the press, the commutation of tithes, and prison reform, as well as the usual party issues of financial retrenchment and curtailment of royal power. In 1819, Smith wrote to Lord Grey:

What I want to see the state do is to lessen in these sad times some of their numerous enemies. Why not do something for the Catholics and scratch them off the list? Then come the Protestant Dissenters. Then of measures,—a mitigation of the game-laws—commutation of tithes —granting to such towns as Birmingham and Manchester the seats in Parliament taken from the rottenness of Cornwall—revision of the Penal Code—sale of the Crown lands—sacrifice of the Droits of Admiralty against a new war.[10]

When the Rector of Foston resumed writing for the *Edinburgh Review*, therefore, it was with a new awareness of the needs of the poor and a determination to be their champion against injustice. One of the most obnoxious measures by which the landed classes used their control of Parliament to legislate for their own benefit was the Game Laws. In order to retain a monopoly on their own pastime, country gentlemen passed a series of laws which restricted shooting to owners of land of one hundred pounds or more a year rental. Persons not so qualified could not shoot game, even at the invitation of a qualified landowner, nor could any game be shot on any piece of land of less value. The sale of game was illegal. Though intended to keep capitalists from shooting on estates which they rented rather than owned, the measures served to encourage poaching. If a rich man wanted a hare or a pheasant to adorn his table, a poor man would provide it. Increasing the punishment for poaching to seven years in an Australian penal colony only made poachers desperate to escape capture, and fatal battles beween poachers and gamekeepers became frequent. The whole series of Game Laws was defended as a means of insuring a large supply of game which would attract country gentlemen to reside at their country seats and so benefit the entire rural neighborhood by their wealth and cultured presence.

As a justice of the peace, Smith saw the harshness of the Game Laws at first hand. He had to sit in judgment upon poachers who were liable to years of exile in a penal colony for snaring a partridge. As often as he could, Smith contrived to set the wretched men free; but most magistrates, shooters themselves, were not so sympathetic, and, as Smith remarked in later years, "for every ten pheasants which fluttered in the wood, one English peasant was rotting in gaol." [11]

His first article on the Game Laws appeared in the *Edinburgh* in March, 1819.[12] He first agrees that it was of great benefit that the aristocracy be somehow lured out of town periodically to attend to the management of their estates and acquaint themselves with the state of the country. He further concedes that game was properly considered private property, though the poacher saw a difference between pigs and partridges. Yet the laws which the squirearchy had enacted to retain a monopoly on game had only resulted in ineffective tyranny. Abolishing qualifications and allowing any man to shoot game on whatever land he owned or rented and to sell that game however he pleased, like any other crop, would put the poacher out of business by setting up lawful competition; and wholesale imprisonment of the English peasantry, as in 1818 when there were twelve hundred convictions for poaching, would be done away with.

The reasoned argumentative approach which Smith takes toward the Game Laws in general changes to bitter ridicule in an article published two years later on the practice of setting spring guns and mantraps to keep off poachers.[13] No advance notice, no provocation, no property rights, he argues, can justify a landowner in putting a man to death for setting foot on his property. There is no question that a squire who hid behind a tree and instantly shot, without warning, anyone who crossed his boundary would be guilty of murder. No matter how widely he published his intention, such homicide is unjustifiable. When the squire was replaced with an automatic mechanism, the guilt was not less, but greater. "A live armigeral spring gun would distinguish an accidental trespasser from a real poacher—a woman or boy from a man—perhaps might spare a friend or an acquaintance—or a father of a family with ten children—or a small freeholder who voted for Administration. But this new rural artillery must destroy, without mercy and selection, every one who approaches it."

Smith brushes aside any argument that the setting of spring guns was meant not to kill or even wound poachers, but merely to act as a deterrent. In that case, he says, there was no need to load the weapons—if only the rumor of their presence or the noise of an occasional detonation was needed. "Against the gun and the powder we have no complaint; . . . our quarrel is with the bullets." But, he claims, those who set loaded guns, whatever their intent, stood ready to kill. "We do not suppose all preservers of game to be so bloodily inclined that they would prefer the death of a poacher to his staying way. Their object is to preserve game; they have no objection to preserve the lives of their fellow-creatures also, if both can exist at the same time; if not, the least worthy of God's creatures must fall—the rustic without a soul, —not the Christian partridge—not the immortal pheasant—not the rational woodcock, or the accountable hare."

In 1823, the Game Laws were investigated by a committee of Parliament, and Smith once more repeated all his arguments to show that severe penalties on poachers had only resulted in misery and bloodshed and that free sale was the only way to eliminate the illegal market.[14] Eventually, his arguments and those of other reformers had their effect. The use of spring guns was made illegal in 1827, and the Game Laws were extensively revised and liberalized in 1831.

IV *Prison Reform*

The Game Laws were only a part of the whole system of criminal and penal law which needed reform. The prisons to which poachers, as well as felons and debtors, were sent were only beginning to be changed from the vice-ridden pestholes they had been for centuries. John Howard had devoted his life to the investigation of penal conditions, visiting prisons in Britain during the 1770's and 1780's, publishing his *State of Prisons in England and Wales* in repeated revisions, and finally dying of a camp-fever in 1790 while studying hospitals in Russia. His work paved the way for a series of reforms. Prisoners were given tolerable food and living conditions, and their health was protected. Debtors and felons, young and old, first offenders and hardened criminals were no longer herded together in common cells.

Although all prison reformers of the early nineteenth century agreed that the first step was to eliminate the cruelty and neglect of the past, there was a major disagreement on what was to replace the old system. Humanitarians wanted prisons to be institutions of rehabilitation, where convicts would be taught religious morality and trades to support them legally after release and would be shown the pleasures of law-abiding society. Elizabeth Fry, the philanthropist who dedicated her life to the guidance and instruction of female convicts, said, "As man is a social being, and not designed for a life of seclusion, such a system of prison discipline [should] be adopted, as may be best to prepare those under its correction, for re-entering active life, and all its consequent exposures and temptations." [15]

Utilitarian thought, on the other hand, held that prisons should serve as institutions of terror to deter crime. Jeremy Bentham, building on the theories of the mid-eighteenth century Italian legal philosopher, Cesare Beccaria, argued that punishment must be harsh enough to offset the pleasures which a criminal stood to gain from his crime; yet, since punishment was an evil in itself, only so harsh as was necessary for it to act as a deterrent. Though the prisoner's well-being was to be constantly guarded from brutality, neglect, or the corruption of greedy officials, convicts must live under conditions equivalent to those of the poorest free and innocent citizens. Bentham's plan for a prison was called the

"Panopticon," a hollow ring of cells which could be observed from a central station by the guards without allowing the prisoners any communication with each other. Work was to be tedious, conversation during work was to be forbidden, and every measure was to be taken to deprive the convict of any opportunity to break the deadly monotony of his existence.

Sydney Smith had a great admiration for the work which Mrs. Fry was doing among the women of the criminal class, and he was once moved to tears when observing her in Newgate. But in a number of articles in the *Edinburgh Review* on prisons, his views are strictly utilitarian.

The first, published in July, 1821, starts with an image that raises indignation rather than pity.[16]

There are, in every county in England, large public schools, maintained at the expense of the county, for the encouragement of profligacy and vice, and for providing a proper succession of housebreakers, profligates, and thieves. . . . The moment any young person evinces the slightest propensity for these pursuits, he is provided with food, clothing, and lodging, and put to his studies under the most accomplished thieves and cut-throats the county can supply.

And although Smith points out that every effort to amend the filth, cruelty, and horror of prisons has been made over the hardhearted and fat-witted objections of vested interest, the vast bulk of his argument is directed against the erroneous reforms of the present rather than the barbarism of the past.

His main objection to the humanitarian approach to prison reform is that it mistakes the purpose of incarceration by seeking to rehabilitate the convicted criminal rather than to frighten the potential lawbreaker.

It is quite obvious that, if men were to appear again, six months after they were hanged, handsomer, richer, and more plump than before execution, the gallows would cease to be an object of terror. But here are men who come out of gaol and say, 'Look at us—we can read and write, we can make baskets and shoes, and we went in ignorant of everything: and we have learnt to do without strong liquors, and have no longer any objection to work; and we did work in the gaol, and have saved money, and here it is.' What is there of terror and detriment in all this? and how are crimes to be lessened if they are thus rewarded?

Smith seems unaware of the amount of credit he gives, in this passage, to the good effects of rehabilitation; or, if he is aware of it, he thinks it irrelevant. For he goes on to propose that the way to effect proper deterrents to crime is to regulate the prisons so that their inmates will have nothing to do but work and repent. Work should be monotonous and tedious, such as treadmill-walking, oakum-picking, brick-pounding. Sentences could be even shorter through solitary imprisonment, a few months of which, part spent in darkness on a coarse diet of bread and water, would be more terrifying than a few years spent in idleness and in the company of other prisoners, eating and drinking whatever could be afforded by the convict.

The importance of food during imprisonment is constantly emphasized by Smith. In 1819, he had written to Lord Lansdowne, who was on a committee investigating prison reform bills, that, "A jail is not an object of terror if men have friends who send them money, and so purchase roast veal and porter." [17] In the *Edinburgh Review*, he recommended that part of the sentence in every criminal case should prescribe the diet of the prisoner, and that no convict, whatever his means, should be allowed to purchase other food.

The next article which Smith wrote on prison reform, a half year after the first, repeats most of his arguments.[18] The review was prompted by a report of the Society for the Improvement of Prison Discipline, an organization whose intentions Smith heartily applauds but whose methods he deplores. He points out that the claims of success which the Society makes, on the basis of decreased recommitments, are the results of fallacious reasoning. The purpose of imprisonment is to keep the prisoner from returning to prison, it is true; but this must be done by punishment, not by reformation. Teaching convicts to weave or cobble may turn them from crime, but it will not prevent others from breaking the law. The success which the Society sees in the decline of second offenses is more than offset by an increase in new commitments, which Smith interprets as caused by a lessened fear of imprisonment.

Smith displayed similar views in regard to the penal colony in Australia. In an article on Botany Bay, written soon after his prison-reform essays, he complains of the practice of selling the labor of convicts as if they were free laborers.

The greatest possible inattention or ignorance appears to have prevailed in manumitting convicts for labour—and for *such* labour! not for cleansing Augean stables, or draining Pontine marshes, or damming out a vast length of the Adriatic, but for working five weeks with a single horse and cart in making the road to Bathurst Plains. . . . Is this comment upon transportation to be circulated in the cells of Newgate, or in the haunts of those persons who are doomed to inhabit them? [19]

V *Judges and Juries*

There is an apparent paradox in Sydney Smith's tender feelings for the poacher and harsh demands upon the convict. However, both were produced by the same utilitarian principles. Though the humanitarian approach to penology eventually won out over the utilitarian, as prisons were made more and more into institutions of rehabilitation by the early twentieth century, the utilitarian philosophy made great improvements in reforming the laws under which men were sent to prison. By viewing punishment strictly as a deterrent, rather than as either reform or revenge, the Benthamites sought a precise, almost mathematical, correlation between the good of society and the evil inflicted on the criminal. The more certain punishment could be made, the more effective it would be as a deterrent, and the less justification there would be for capital punishment. The indiscriminate use of the death penalty in repeated attempts to curb the rising crime rate of seventeenth- and eighteenth-century England had led, by the nineteenth century, to the classification of over two hundred crimes as capital offenses. This resulted not only in punishment cruelly out of proportion to the crime but also in the acquittal of many obviously guilty defendants whom juries refused to send to the gallows for petty offenses.

Abatement of capital punishment was only one part of the utilitarian program of legal reform. In order to justify strictly punitive, rather than rehabilitative, imprisonment, it was vital that the trial and conviction of those accused of crimes be scrupulously fair. Sydney Smith had occasion to write against a misapplication of the principles of punitive imprisonment soon after he had expressed those very principles in the *Edinburgh*. In the North Riding of Yorkshire, the local magistrates ruled that prisoners indicted and awaiting trial, who could neither raise bail nor purchase their own food, should be compelled to work on the treadmill for their support. This was so apparently a violation of the principle that the accused is innocent until proven guilty, that Smith's arguments seem remarkable only because they had to be made at all.[20] The treadmill, he points out, is punishment by tedious labor, perfectly suited to render the life of a convict hard, but not to be forced on a supposedly innocent man as an alternative to starvation. The effect of the ruling was that a man was imprisoned because he was accused and punished because he was poor.

A and B are accused of some bailable offense. A has no bail to offer; and no money to support himself in prison, and therefore, his four or five months in the treadmill. B gives bail, appears at his trial, and both are sentenced to two months' imprisonment. In this case the one suffers three times as much as the other for the same offense: but suppose A is acquitted and B found guilty,—the innocent man has then laboured five months because he was poor, and the guilty man labours two months because he was rich.

The distinction before the law between rich and poor and the confusion of accused and convicted was the subject of Smith's last *Edinburgh* essay on the treatment of criminals. The English law did not allow persons indicted for felony the benefit of counsel in their defense except to argue on points of law. The defendant's attorney, if there were one, could not introduce the case, examine or cross-examine witnesses, nor sum up to the jury. In 1826, Smith wrote an argument for giving a man on trial for a felony the same advantages offered to defendants in cases of civil disputes, misdemeanor, and treason.[21] He had introduced the topic briefly into his first article on prisons and at greater length in his second; when he made it the subject of a separate review, he wrote the best of his articles on criminal and penal law. His argument was stronger than those on prison reform, because he was calling not merely for utility, but for humanity. The issue was more pressing than that of the treatment of untried prisoners in Yorkshire, because the injustice was not one perpetrated by a few local magistrates as an innovation but an old abuse originating in feudal subservience to the crown and defended by those who called the tyranny of the past the wisdom of their ancestors.

The origins of this injustice, Smith said, were in the medieval belief that defense of the accused implied disloyalty to the King. In civil cases, where the Crown was not a party; in misdemeanor, where the offense was less serious; and in treason, where the accused were generally of the higher classes, it was assumed that the best way for a true verdict to be reached was for opposing attorneys each to present evidence and interpret it to the jury in order to throw the strongest possible light on his side of the case. Only in felony was the defendant, usually poor and illiterate and never trained in the law, left to defend himself against the power and skill of the prosecution as best he could.

The inequities are obvious. Smith cites the hypothetical case of leaders of a mob demonstration who refuse to disperse after warning by the magistrates. They could be indicted for levying war against the King, a form of treason, or for seditious rioting, a misdemeanor. But the Crown could, if it chose, try them for violation of the Riot Act, a felony, and effectively prosecute for a death penalty without having to contend with defense counsel. Smith continues,

It produces, in many other cases disconnected with treason, the most scandalous injustice. A receiver of stolen goods, who employs a young girl to rob her master, may be tried for the misdemeanour; the young girl taken afterwards would be tried for the felony. The receiver would be punished only with fine, imprisonment, or whipping, and he could have counsel to defend him. The girl indicted for felony, and liable to death, would enjoy no such advantage.

Although Smith's arguments on the inequity of the law in operation are somewhat weakened by his use of such extremely specific hypothetical illustrations, his arguments against those who defended the practice are both general and effective. He scorns as hypocritical the usual arguments raised in favor of denying counsel to prisoners. He concedes that most of those indicted were guilty, but he says that the number of last-minute reprieves from

the gallows showed that innocent men were occasionally convicted and only proven innocent when generous individuals, after
the trial, did what an attorney could have done during it. How
many innocent convicts were never vindicated? How many prisoners, convicted to imprisonment rather than death, could never stir
enough interest to get such help? The pious concern for the prisoner's welfare that sought to spare him the expense of an attorney's fee was nonsense, for what could be more expensive than
being hanged, especially when the Crown confiscated the property
of convicted felons? How could defendants of the ancient tyranny
say that the judge acted as attorney for the accused, when the
judge could neither interview the prisoner nor interpret evidence
partially?

The real reason for the continuance of the practice was that
felonies, among which scores were capital offenses, were the do-
main of the poor. The wealthy and powerful who controlled the
legislature made sure that in civil suits or cases of treason or misdemeanor, in which they might be defendants, counsel was allowed on both sides. Why was there no great public outcry
against the injustice? Why were there not innumerable bills
brought before the House?

To ask why there are not petitions—why the evil is not more noticed,
is mere parliamentary froth and ministerial juggling. Gentlemen are
rarely hung. If they were so, there would be petitions without end
for counsel. . . . Let two gentlemen on the Ministerial side of the
House (we only ask for two) commit some crimes which will render
their execution a matter of painful necessity. Let them feel, and report
to the House, all the injustice and inconvenience of having neither a
copy of the indictment, nor a list of witnesses, nor counsel to defend
them.

VI   *The Tyranny of Wealth*

It was not only in the treatment of criminals that Sydney Smith
showed his tendency for reform and his humanity. In 1814, he
applauded the work of the Society of Friends in establishing an
asylum for the insane founded on principles of kind treatment
rather than brutal confinement.[22] And, in 1822, he praised the
medical profession for its fight against smallpox by vaccination,
a technique still rather uncertain and widely suspected twenty

[113]

years after Jenner's discoveries had been accepted and rewarded by the British government.[23]

However, when Smith turned his attention from the position of the poor and weak under the injustices of law and custom to their position under the tyranny of wealth, his liberalism was less marked. An 1819 article upon chimney sweepers opens with a memorable passage:[24]

An excellent and well-arranged dinner is a most pleasing occurrence, and a great triumph of civilized life. It is not only the descending morsel, and the enveloping sauce—but the rank, wealth, wit, and beauty which surround the meats—the learned management of light and heat—the silent and rapid services of the attendants—the smiling and sedulous host, proffering gusts and relishes—the exotic bottle— the embossed plate—the pleasant remarks—the handsome dresses— the cunning artifices in fruit and farina! The hour of dinner, in short, includes every thing of sensual and intellectual gratification which a great nation glories in producing.

In the midst of all this, who knows that the kitchen chimney caught fire half an hour before dinner!—and that a poor little wretch, of six or seven years old, was sent up in the midst of the flames to put it out?

Despite this beginning, Smith seems to have more real sympathy for the luxuries which he mocks than the sufferings for which he weeps. After quoting pages of parliamentary reports revealing the brutality with which sweeps are treated by masters and the frequency of suffocation, burning, cancer, and crippling among boys sent into the trade, Smith concludes, in a section apparently devoid of qualifying irony:

After all, we must own that it was quite right to throw out the bill for prohibiting the sweeping of chimneys by boys—because humanity is a modern invention; and there are many chimneys in old houses which cannot possibly be swept in any other manner. . . . We should have been very glad to have seconded the views of the Climbing Society, and have pleaded for the complete abolition of climbing boys, if we could conscientiously have done so. But such a measure, we are convinced from the evidence, could not be carried into execution without great injury to property, and increased risk of fire.

This same Whiggish commitment to the interests of property is to be found in the two articles which Smith wrote for the

Edinburgh, in 1820 and 1821, on the Poor Laws.[25] The bulk of these reviews is taken up with criticism of the various reforms proposed to replace the tangle of local regulations governing parish relief of the indigent; and a great many technical points are made about the possible effects of new regulations for settlement of paupers, periodic labor needs, litigation among towns, and so forth. A few principles guide Smith's thoughts on Poor Laws in general. First, they are an unwarranted tax upon property; secondly, they encourage the lower classes to have far too many children and to depend on the parish to support them in idleness; and third, poor relief must be gradually abolished.

In 1834, a New Poor Law was adopted abolishing all out-of-door doles in the parishes and forcing the poor who wanted relief to enter centrally administered workhouses intentionally designed to be so wretched that paupers would choose any alternative to them but absolute starvation. Far from commenting on the harshness of the system, which followed the principles he himself endorsed for prisons, Smith merely appended a note to his Poor Law articles in his collected works of 1839, deploring only the rashness of acting so quickly that general discontent might turn to general disorder.[26] In the same year, the last part of *Oliver Twist* was published in *Bentley's Miscellany,* exposing the misery of workhouse paupers who were caught between the coldly scientific indifference of the utilitarians who had formulated the New Poor Law, and the deliberate neglect and cruelty of the local guardians who opposed it.

Sydney Smith once said of the utilitarians, "That school treat mankind as if they were mere machines; the feelings or affections never enter into their calculations. If every thing is to be sacrificed to utility, why do you bury your grandmother at all: why don't you cut her into small pieces at once, and make portable soup of her?"[27] Yet Smith was in agreement with the Benthamites on social and legal questions far more often than not. His views on prisons, poor relief, education, and state religion coincided almost exactly with those of the utilitarians. He shared with the Benthamites an attachment to the associationist school of British empirical philosophy and to the legal philosophy of Cesare Beccaria, whose work he studied in preparation for service as a justice of the peace. When dealing with his family or his rural parishioners, his warmth and sympathy resulted in works of compassion and humanity. But in dealing with the vast, nameless, statistical mass of "the people," Smith yielded his natural feelings to the iron laws of classical economics and utilitarian sociology.

The shortcomings of his social philosophy are most apparent when his treatment of the Poor Law is compared with that in *Oliver Twist*, when his praise of Lancaster's method of disciplining pupils by shaming them is compared with the picture of David Copperfield wearing a placard, "Take care of him. He bites," upon his back, and when his recommendations for prison reform are compared with the description of the horrors of solitary confinement in *American Notes*. Yet if reformers like Sydney Smith had not fought in their generation for systematic treatment of paupers, education of the lower classes, and just treatment of prisoners, however many faults there were in their programs and whatever their limited notion of what constituted the interests of the nation, Charles Dickens and his contemporaries could not have added compassion to science in the social reforms of the age which followed.

CHAPTER 6

Across the Atlantic

I Philoyankeeist

"MY DEAR Jeffrey," wrote Sydney Smith on November 23, 1818, "I entirely agree with you respecting the Americans, and believe that I am to the full as much of a Philoyankeeist as you are. I doubt if there ever was an instance of a new people conducting their affairs with so much wisdom, or if there ever was such an extensive scene of human happiness and prosperity."[1] Smith, with his literary acquaintances of the *Edinburgh Review* and his social and political friends of Holland House, belonged to the small minority of Britons who admired the example of liberty and progress set by the handful of insurgent colonies across the Atlantic.

Lord Holland had met James Monroe in 1806, at a conference on Anglo-American maritime differences and had maintained a correspondence with him through Monroe's two terms as President. In 1823, Lord Holland wrote that in the forty years since America had won its independence, "almost every monarchy in Christendom has been convulsed by insurrections, revolutions and changes, but the Republic of the United States has been uniformly tranquil and undisturbed in its sure progress, improvement and prosperity."[2]

The *Edinburgh Review*, almost alone among British periodicals, treated American subjects and American books fairly, without automatically sneering at anything from the United States. The experiment in democracy which had started in Philadelphia in 1776 had been too violently and dangerously imitated in France for the majority of Britons to view it with any attitude but fear and scorn. With the reactionism of the Tory government, first to Jacobinism and then to radicalism, coloring their judgment, Englishmen could hardly sympathize with the fortunes of a country which had been born from their blood and in defiance of their rule. Throughout the first half of the nineteenth century, scores of prejudiced British travelers went to America and returned to report what their prejudice had seen. The vast majority of travel books were violently anti-American, disparaging new world manners, morals, and institutions. Americans, by the same token, were extremely suspicious of anything English and touchy about criticism. Fiercely nationalistic, the American press answered British critics in such books as *An Appeal from the Judgments of Great Britain respecting the United States* (1819), by Robert Walsh, and *John Bull in America; or, the New Munchausen* (1825), by James Kirke Paulding, as well as in newspapers and magazines. Mrs. Trollope's *Domestic Manners of the Americans* (1832) and Charles Dickens' *American Notes* (1842) were later attacks in a long tradition of Anglo-American literary warfare. Yet, throughout this period, the *Edinburgh Review* was outspoken against such one-sided travel books, and none of the reviewers was a better friend to the United States than Sydney Smith.

The position of the *Edinburgh,* and of Smith, can be most clearly seen in contrast to that of the *Quarterly Review,* which for many years could not find anything good to say about America. For example, in a review of a volume of American travels, the *Quarterly* calls the author, Henry Bradshaw Fearon, "a democratic fieffé," blind to any merits of England or faults of the United States, and ready to believe all the anti-British talk he encountered in his travels.[3] Yet, in the same month, Smith described Fearon's work to Lord Grey as, "a clever book but hardly fair to America."[4] The month before, Smith had published his first article on America in the *Edinburgh Review.*[5] Fearon is one of the authors reviewed, and is described as, "a much abler writer than [John Palmer or John Bradbury, other travelers whose books are reviewed], but no lover of America—and a little given to exaggeration in his views of vices and prejudices."

However, rather than dwelling upon the faults of Mr. Fearon, Smith devotes his article to praising a number of the political and social institutions of the United States. Freedom of speech and opposition he considers one great advantage which the United States has over Britain. When the New England states opposed and tried to thwart the war effort of 1812, Jefferson and

Madison relied on public opinion to support the government, rather than resorting to trials for seditious libel and suspension of the Habeas Corpus Act, as the timid British government had done in similar circumstances.

There are other, more day-to-day advantages of American democracy which Smith admires. The low cost of American government, free from aristocratic jobbery and archaic sinecures, calls for an envious look. And the low salaries of public officials are only representative of the whole nature of an equalitarian society. Smith quotes a passage from one of the travel books describing the simplicity of dinner at the home of an "ex-King," John Adams; baked Indian pudding in an eight-room house offers a great contrast to the expensive luxuries of the English aristocracy. Law, too, is cheap; and stripped of wigs, robes, and other trappings, American courts can do better than those in Britain, where it is often less expensive to give up a claim than to sue for it. Religious toleration and the lack of an establishment have allowed a wide variety of churches to spring up in America, and rather than producing indifference toward religion, freedom of faith has made the country very devout.

The great drawback to the reputation of the United States, the one great stain on her character, is slavery. "We wish well to America—we rejoice in her prosperity—and are delighted to resist the absurd impertinence with which the character of her people is often treated in this country: but the existence of slavery in America is an atrocious crime, with which no measures can be kept—for which her situation affords no sort of apology—which makes liberty itself distrusted, and the boast of it disgusting."

In 1820, Smith wrote a second article on America, reviewing Adam Seybert's *Statistical Annals of the United States of America*.[6] In summarizing the many facts and figures with which Seybert's work is crammed, Smith points out the amazing growth in population, cultivated land, commerce, and revenue of the United States. Smith again comments on the economy with which the American government is run in comparison with the British, and he warns his American readers against seeking military and naval glory lest the expense ruin them. He cites the example of the hapless Briton, oppressed by

TAXES upon every article which enters into the mouth, or covers the back, or is placed under the foot—taxes upon every thing which it is pleasant to see, hear, feel, smell, or taste—taxes upon warmth, light, and locomotion—taxes on every thing on earth, and the waters under the earth—on every thing that comes from abroad, or is grown at home —taxes on the raw material—taxes on every fresh value that is added to it by the industry of man—taxes on the sauce which pampers man's appetite, and the drug that restores him to health—on the ermine which decorates the judge, and the rope which hangs the criminal— on the poor man's salt, and the rich man's spice—on the brass nails of the coffin, and the ribands of the bride—at bed or board, couchant or levant, we must pay.—The schoolboy whips his taxed top—the beard-less youth manages his taxed horse, with a taxed bridle, on a taxed road:—and the dying Englishman, pouring his medicine, which has paid 7 per cent. into a spoon that has paid 15 per cent.—flings himself back upon his chintz bed, which has paid 22 per cent.—and expires in the arms of an apothecary who has paid a licence of a hundred pounds for the privilege of putting him to death. His whole property is then immediately taxed from 2 to 10 per cent. Besides the probate, large fees are demanded for burying him in the chancel; his virtues are handed down to posterity on taxed marble; and he is then gathered to his fathers—to be taxed no more.

In 1824, Smith found even more to admire in American institu-tions.[7] In his third and last article on the United States for the *Edinburgh Review,* he again contrasts British jobbery with Amer-ican economy in government and goes on to praise the freedom with which American merchants are able to trade all over the world unencumbered by the tax and tariff restrictions of Britain. Most of all, he praises the attention given in the United States to popular education. He mentions the provisions of the North-west Ordinance of 1787 (though he does not mention the law by name) which allowed for public education in all new public lands. He points out the beginnings of the state university system, and he calculates what the size of America's investment in educa-tion will be by the time all the western lands are settled. These facts, he says, "quite put into the back-ground every thing which had been done in the Old World for the improvement of the lower orders, and confer deservedly upon the Americans the char-acter of a wise, a reflecting, and a virtuous people."

II   *American Bards and a Scotch Reviewer*

The inevitable discomforts to be found in a new country, sparsely populated and just emerging from the wilderness, Smith considers negligible compared with the success of popular government. In his third article, he concludes:

America seems, on the whole, to be a country possessing vast advantages, and little inconveniences; they have a cheap government, and bad roads; they pay no tithes, and have stage coaches without springs. They have no poor laws and no monopolies—but their inns are inconvenient and travellers are teased with questions. They have no collections in the fine arts; but they have no Lord Chancellor, and they can go to law without absolute ruin. They cannot make Latin verses, but they expend immense sums in the education of the poor. In all this the balance is prodigiously in their favour.

Among the "little inconveniences" which Smith mentions is a lack of culture. In his first article on America, he states that there is next to no native American literature.

There is, or was, a Mr. Dwight, who wrote some poems; and his baptismal name was Timothy. There is also a small account of Virginia by Jefferson, and an epic by Joel Barlow: and some pieces of pleasantry by Mr. Irving. But why should the Americans write books, when a six weeks' passage brings them, in their own tongue, our sense, science, and genius, in bales and hogsheads? Prairies, steam-boats, grist-mills, are their natural objects for centuries to come. Then, when they have got to the Pacific Ocean—epic poems, plays, pleasures of memory, and all the elegant gratifications of an ancient people who have tamed the wild earth, and set down to amuse themselves.—This is the natural march of human affairs.

In his second article, Smith points out that there is a tendency in American journals to praise all American culture indiscriminately, when America is patently most cultured in its British heritage.

In the four quarters of the globe, who reads an American book? or goes to an American play? or looks at an American picture or statue? What does the world yet owe to American physicians or surgeons? What new substances have their chemists discovered? or what old ones have they analysed? What new constellations have been discovered by the tele-scopes of Americans? What have they done in the mathematics? Who drinks out of American glasses? or eats from American plates? or wears American coats or gowns? or sleeps in American blankets?

When Smith makes gentle fun of American vulgarities, whether dialectic speech or rural curiosity, it is with the understanding that such things are to be expected in a new country and are venial at worst, perhaps even commendable as a means of promot-ing national unity and communal spirit. But the pretense of the United States to any level of literary culture comparable to that of England aroused only his scorn. He respected Franklin, and once told a young friend, playfully, "I will disinherit you if you do not admire everything written by Franklin";[8] but the sage of Philadelphia, after all, was a product of British letters and thought. The notion of a worthy native American literature, re-flecting the new republic's ideas and independent of English tra-dition, was what Smith could not accept.

The American press was very touchy about British criticism, and even Jeffrey was unwilling to risk offending if he could avoid it. In his own review of Joel Barlow's *Columbiad* in 1809, Jeffrey damns the epic as thoroughly as he had treated less ambitious works by better poets.[9] But in his opening paragraph he points out that the faults of the poet are not those of his entire nation. "The truth however is, that though the American *government* be new, the *people* is in all respects as old as the people of England; and their want of literature is to be ascribed, not to the immaturity of their progress in civilization, but to the nature of the occupa-tions in which they are generally engaged." Jeffrey is saying, essentially, exactly what Smith later said about American culture, but doing it in much more flattering terms. And rather than con-demn all American art and industry as second rate, Jeffrey, at the conclusion of his attack on Barlow, notes the beauty of the book itself, commenting on the fine quality of print, paper, and binding as indicative of high standards in craftsmanship and the growing taste of the American reading public.

That Jeffrey's private views corresponded to Smith's public ones can be seen from a letter of 1815 to his father-in-law, Charles

Wilkes of New York. "You are too desponding as to the future prospects of America," Jeffrey says. "She will breed an aristocracy by-and-by, and then you will get rid of all your vulgar miseries." [10] But the *Edinburgh Review* was too popular in America and too strong a champion of the United States for him to allow such views to creep into its pages. In 1822, Smith started to review a book by an American author but dropped the article, three-fourths completed, when Jeffrey insisted that Smith reduce such raillery as would offend American cultural ego.[11]

Jeffrey was wise to avoid collision with American cultural claims. Smith's query, "Who reads an American book?" raised such resentment against him in the United States that he commented in his third article on America:

It is rather surprising that such a people, spreading rapidly over so vast a portion of the earth, and cultivating all the liberal and useful arts so successfully, should be so extremely sensitive and touchy as the Americans are said to be. We really thought at one time they would have fitted out an armament against the Edinburgh and Quarterly Reviews, and burnt down Mr. Murray's and Mr. Constable's shops, as we did the American Capitol. We, however, remember no other anti-American crime of which we were guilty, than a preference of Shakespeare and Milton over Joel Barlow and Timothy Dwight. That opinion we must still take the liberty of retaining.

Smith's question was certainly not prompted by poor literary judgment; in 1820 very few people in Europe did read American books. At worst, it was ill-timed; for within a year after it was posed, Irving's *Sketch Book,* Cooper's *Spy,* and Bryant's *Poems* were beginning to gain international recognition for native American literature. But literary judgment had little to do with the resentment Smith's comment raised in the United States. If British criticism of the period was overeager to belittle American culture, American criticism was even more chauvinistic in its claims for native talent. Smith's words became a perennial challenge to American literary patriots. An essay by Poe, first published in 1842, shows not only how justified Smith's words had been in 1820 but also how familiar they had remained for twenty-two years.

Among all the *pioneers* of American literature, whether prose or poetical, there is *not one* whose productions have not been much overrated by his countrymen. . . . In the first place, we have but to consider that gratitude, surprise, and a species of hyper-patriotic triumph have been blended, and finally confounded with mere admiration, or appreciation, in respect to the labors of our earlier writers; . . . [But] there is no longer reason or wit in the query,—"Who reads an American book?" [12]

III *The Pennsylvania Debts*

In the same year that Poe's essay appeared, quoting the two-decade-old statement which had earned Smith so much enmity in the United States, a new cause of friction between Smith and America arose. Many of the states, emulating the success of New York in building a canal from the Hudson to the Great Lakes, had undertaken the construction of roads and canals by selling bonds. In 1842 and 1843, a general recession reduced a number of states to defaulting on the payment of dividends, and others, including Pennsylvania, repudiated their debts altogether. Wordsworth was among the cheated creditors of Pennsylvania and displayed his wrath, early in 1845, in a blistering sonnet "To the Pennsylvanians."

> ~~~~~ undefiled by luxury or sloth,
> Firm self-denial, manners grave and staid,
> Rights equal, laws with cheerfulness obeyed,
> Words that require no sanction from an oath,
> And simple honesty a common growth—
> This high repute, with bounteous Nature's aid,
> Won confidence, now ruthlessly betrayed
> At will, your power the measure of your troth!—
> All who revere the memory of Penn
> Grieve for the land on whose wild woods his name
> Was fondly grafted with a virtuous aim,
> Renounced, abandoned by degenerate Men
> For state-dishonour black as ever came
> To upper air from Mammon's loathsome den.[13]

Smith was another investor in Pennsylvania bonds. His loss was not a heavy one, but his public protest came earlier than Wordsworth's and drew a great deal more attention to itself.

In a petition to the Congress of the United States, Smith asked that some measures be taken, "for the restoration of American credit, and for the repayment of debts incurred and repudiated by several of the States." Since the repudiation had been caused by neither war nor any other natural or man-made catastrophe, and since the roads and canals for which the money had been borrowed were actually in operation, Pennsylvania's refusal to pay on its bonds could only be construed as a lack of good faith incompatible with the high moral standards the United States had set for itself.

Your Petitioner sincerely prays that the great and good men still existing among you may, by teaching to the United States the deep disgrace they have incurred in the whole world, restore them to moral health, to that high position they have lost, and which, for the happiness of mankind, it is so important they should ever maintain; for the United States are now working out the greatest of political problems, and upon that confederacy the eyes of thinking men are intensely fixed, to see how far the mass of mankind can be trusted with the management of their own affairs, and the establishment of their own happiness.

The petition was, of course, of no legislative value, for the Federal Congress, even if it had wanted to, could not make Pennsylvania pay. But Smith's intentions, as usual, were not to influence lawmakers but to influence public opinion. He had the petition published in the London *Morning Chronicle* on May 18, 1843, and it was widely reprinted in the United States. On November 3 and November 22 of the same year, he published letters on the subject of the American debts in the *Chronicle*, and then he republished all three items in the form of a pamphlet.[14]

In the two letters which followed the petition, Smith employed a more familiar kind of rhetoric than the ornate style and humble tone with which he had addressed Congress.

In every grammar-school of the old world *ad Græcas Calendas*[15] is translated—the American dividends. . . .

Figure to yourself a Pennsylvanian receiving foreigners in his own country, walking over the public works with them, and showing them Larcenous Lake, Swindling Swamp, Crafty Canal, and Rogues' Railway, and other dishonest works. "This swamp we gained (says the patriotic borrower) by the repudiated loan of 1828. Our canal robbery was in 1830; we pocketed your good people's money for the railroad only last year."

Sydney Smith's war with the Commonwealth of Pennsylvania attracted wide notice. On December 18, 1843, he wrote to a friend, "My bomb has fallen very successfully in America, and the list of killed and wounded is extensive. I have several quires of paper sent me every day, calling me monster, thief, atheist, deist, etc." [16] Not all of the reaction from the United States was against Smith. Many Americans wrote to him to support his plea for honesty; numerous gifts—apples, cheese, and such—arrived from American admirers who wanted to atone in part for the sins of their countrymen. And one important segment of the American press, the Boston literary circle, came to his defense. In 1815, Edward Everett and George Ticknor had met Smith and the rest of the *Edinburgh Review* circle while studying in Europe. Everett edited the *North American Review* for a number of years before he left his professorship at Harvard for a political career, and Ticknor, also a professor at Harvard, remained an influential critic throughout his life. The Boston literati were the least chauvinistic of Americans about native literature and were also the first to recognize the justice of Smith's attack on Pennsylvania.

Everett, who was Minister Plenipotentiary to England at the time of the debt controversy, later said of Smith, "If he had not been known as the wittiest man of his day, he would have been accounted one of the wisest." [17] And Ticknor, writing in the Boston *Advertiser*, pointed out that the bitterness of Smith's letters on Pennsylvania resulted from the truth of his charge of dishonesty, rather than from any intent to be malicious. After sketching Smith's long career as a polemicist for free institutions, Ticknor added:

The Rev. Sydney Smith is, after all, only the representative of a very large class of men, . . . of moderate property and much intelligence [, who] have had greater confidence in free institutions than the rich and powerful around them. They have looked upon us Americans especially with kindness, respect, and cheerful trust; when others, of more worldly consideration than themselves, have looked upon us with aversion and contempt. They have been, in short, our sincere friends; . . . And how have we requited their confidence? Mr. Smith's petition may inform us.[18]

IV *American Reputation*

The battle over Pennsylvania bonds only affected Sydney Smith's American reputation for a short time. When an American edition of his collected works appeared in 1844, once more bringing him to attention in the United States, the *North American Review* noted that Smith's attack on the dishonesty of Americans was no different from his many previous attacks on similar faults of the English, and that Smith was no prejudiced libeler but a shrewd, honest, independent, and amusing man who denounced fraud wherever he found it.[19] Twelve years later, when reviewing Saba Holland's *Memoir,* the same journal remarked, "Notwithstanding the deserved rebuke he administered to our national delinquency in his American letters, he vindicated his claim to the title of Philo-Yankeeist. No British writer has better appreciated the institutions and destiny of the United States." [20] A New York publication complained that Americans knew Smith only for the Pennsylvania letters and associated him with the many British tourists and writers who had lambasted the United States. "Why," the article states, "Sydney Smith is the old protector of [this] country in the Edinburgh Review, from these very assailants." [21]

Pennsylvanians were slower to forgive and forget. An obituary notice of Smith which appeared in *Godey's Ladies Book* (a Philadelphia publication) in 1846 ends, "Upon the whole, we conclude Mr. Smith to have been a keen-witted and sensible worldling, more capable of discerning the faults and absurdities of others than desirous of correcting his own." [22] And even when Saba Holland's *Memoir* appeared in the United States, and the *Church Review* of New Haven predicted that it would lessen American bitterness against Smith,[23] another Philadelphia journal, the *Princeton Review,* took every opportunity to distort, misquote, and even speculate in order to vilify Smith.[24] But by then almost all of the indebted states had long since paid off their creditors, and most Americans were in a position to agree with the man who had berated their previous dishonesty.

However, Smith's attack upon the cultural claims of the United States was not forgotten. "Who reads an American book?" remained the one quotation from Smith most often remembered in the United States. In 1876, *The Nation* cited this passage to show that Smith had been the author of "savagely contemptuous articles about America," full of "ill-natured gibes and jeers."[25] A 1930 American doctoral dissertation, intended to prove the *Edinburgh Review* the champion of the United States in the British press, used many quotations from Smith's three articles to show the *Edinburgh*'s pro-Americanism. These were not identified as Smith's but merely as from the journal. Only the passage, "Who reads an American book?", was tagged with Smith's name.[26] And on March 17, 1963, a CBS television program called "Creative America" was introduced as a reply to Smith's one hundred and forty-three year old "sneering" comment.

That Sydney Smith's remarks on American culture were prompted by rational analysis and sincere good will rather than by insular prejudice or spite can be shown by comparing his articles on the United States with those on Australia. He saw in "Newgate, then become a quarter of the world," a new America, colonized, used for penal transportation, and fast becoming a nation in its own right. He equated the two countries politically, and insisted that a more liberal view of colonial rights must be taken if Australia were to become independent through British policy rather than despite it. As early as 1803, he said, "It may be a curious consideration, to reflect what we are to do with this colony when it comes to years of discretion. Are we to spend another hundred millions of money in discovering its strength, and to humble ourselves again before a fresh set of Washingtons and Franklins?"[27]

It is only reasonable to expect that, if Smith had intended to attack the United States as an upstart nation which had no right to thrive once it had the impertinence to leave the British Empire, he would have found the example of loyal Australia a convenient whip to use against America. But rather than emphasizing the differences between the republic and the colony, he noted many points of similarity, and he criticized the cultural pretensions of Australians as he had those of Americans. In 1819, he confessed himself "considerably amused" by the self-importance of Australian society as seen in the social and fashionable news of hunts, cattle sales, new coaches, and racing found in a colonial newspaper which could not even publish regularly because the supply of paper was uncertain.[28]

As in America, and even more so because Australia was newer, attention had to be given to the useful arts before the elegant ones. An inquiry made by Parliament into the conduct of the Governor of New South Wales in 1822 revealed, among other things, that ornamental architecture had been encouraged. Smith exclaimed, "Ornamental architecture in Botany Bay! How it could enter into the head of any human being to adorn public buildings at the Bay, or to aim at any other architectural purpose but the exclusion of wind and rain, we are utterly at a loss to conceive. Such an expense is not only lamentable for the waste of property it makes in the particular instance, but because it destroys that guarantee of sound sense which the Government at home must require in those who preside over distant colonies." [29]

As well as seeing American faults in Australia, Smith saw American virtues there. Although he said that the underdeveloped and underpopulated nature of the country made such free institutions as trial by jury and representative legislature impractical for a while, because of difficulties of communication and lack of leisure among the citizens, his greatest hope for the colony was that, by a policy of gradual manumission rather than by bloodshed and bitterness, it might someday become as independent and free a republic as the United States. Smith noted that in the provision of education for the lower classes Australia already showed promise of following the example of America in building a free society.

What greater praise could a nation want than to be held up as a model to future countries? Smith was so devoted to championing the cause of the United States against British prejudice that he felt obliged to append a note to his 1824 article on America, reading:

Ancient women, whether in or out of breeches, will of course imagine that we are the enemies of the institutions of our country, because we are the admirers of the institutions of America: but circumstances differ. American institutions are too new, English institutions are ready made to our hands. *If we were to build the house afresh, we might perhaps avail ourselves of the improvements of a new plan;* but we have no sort of wish to pull down an excellent house, strong, warm, and comfortable, because, upon second trial we might be able to alter and amend it.[30]

This is, of course, the Whig speaking for preservation of the old framework. However, the Whig was never the rabid anti-American. Yet, in *Webster's Biographical Dictionary*, Sydney Smith is still described as a "denouncer of everything American." In simple justice, if not in appreciation, he deserves a better reputation in the United States than that.

CHAPTER 7

Literary Criticism

I A *Literate Gentleman*

OF ALL Sydney Smith's essays for the *Edinburgh Review*, only five could strictly be called literary criticism—reviews of one play and four novels.[1] His correspondence, bristling as it is with commentary and opinion on the passing scene in politics, society, and culture, adds little to this meager store. There are a number of letters to Archibald Constable, the publisher, offering comments on some of the Waverley novels,[2] and a lively interchange of letters with T. H. Lister concerning possible subjects of historical tragedy.[3] But for the most part, Smith was a critic of ideas rather than of books.

Even when books themselves became the subject, rather than merely vehicles, of controversy, Smith seemed only partially concerned. When Jeffrey was waging his notorious battle with the Lake poets over the question of what constituted poetry, Smith's comments showed more social than literary awareness. In 1814, Smith wrote to Jeffrey concerning the latter's brutal review of *The Excursion*, "I have not read the review of Wordsworth, because the subject is to me so very uninteresting; but may I ask was it worth while to take any more notice of a man respecting whom the public opinion is completely made up? and do not such repeated attacks upon the man wear in some little degree the shape of persecution?"[4] And Smith's remarks on Jeffrey's review of *Biographia Literaria*, a few years later, are in the same vein. "Jeffrey has thrashed Coleridge happily and deservedly;—but is it not time now to lay up his cudgel? Heads that are plastered and trepanned all over are no longer fit for breaking."[5]

Southey, the third of the Lakers, is barely mentioned in Smith's letters as a poet; the closest Smith came to commenting on the laureate's work was to mention his *Life of Wesley* as a possible subject for a review taking up the old battle against Methodism.

On Shelley and Keats he is entirely silent, although he almost certainly knew of the charges of atheism against the one and of the notorious review of *Endymion* often considered, at the time, a factor in the death of the other.

Smith has somewhat more to say about Byron than about any of the other major Romantic poets; but this is because of social acquaintance rather than for any literary reasons. Smith met Byron frequently in Whig aristocratic circles and gossiped in his letters about Lady Caroline Lamb's attempted suicide, the Byron marriage, and the shocked reception of *Don Juan*. Smith himself was satirized as "Smug Sydney" in *English Bards and Scotch Reviewers* and as "The very powerful parson, Peter Pith,/The loudest wit I e'er was deafen'd with" in *Don Juan*. He thought of Byron as a gentleman who wrote verse rather than as a poet (a view which Byron himself often shared). In a review of a travel book, Smith once remarked, "To publish verses is become a sort of evidence that a man wants sense; which is repelled not by writing good verses, but by writing excellent verses;—by doing what Lord Byron has done." [6]

The contemporary poets with whom Smith was most familiar, those whom he knew socially and whose works always found notice in his correspondence, were Thomas Moore and Samuel Rogers, protégés, like Smith himself, of the aristocracy. Smith felt at home with their polished verse, whether singing Moore's lyrics with his family or reading Rogers' elegant travelogues. Such tastes fit the life of a gentleman, who took literature as part of his life but did not study it as life itself. Lord Houghton said of Smith, "He thought it no more necessary for a man to remember the different books that had made him wise than the different dinners that had made him healthy." [7]

II *The Canons of Judgment*

Although Sydney Smith was not a student of literature, he was, to the extent of five reviews and two series of letters, a literary critic. And, to this extent, he exercised literary judgment based upon a set of literary standards.

The first thing Smith demanded of fiction or drama was pleasure. In his review of T. H. Lister's *Granby*, he says, "The main question as to a novel is—did it amuse? were you surprised at dinner coming so soon? did you mistake eleven for ten, and twelve for eleven? were you too late to dress? and did you sit up beyond the usual hour? If a novel produces these effects, it is good; if it does not—story, language, scandal itself cannot save it. It is only meant to please; and it must do that, or it does nothing." In his letters to Constable on Scott's novels, Smith seems to judge each book according to the charm and novelty of its characters. He disliked Scott's overuse of such comic characters as Meg Merrilies and Dominie Sampson, charming at first but stale after two or three repetitions.

A second standard Smith applied to literature was a didactic one. In reviewing Matthew Gregory "Monk" Lewis's tragedy, *Alphonso, King of Castile*, he objects to the play's immorality with the playful remark, "Ottilia at last becomes quite furious, from the conviction that Cæsario has been sleeping with a second lady, called Estella; whereas he has really been sleeping with a third lady, called Amelrosa. Passing across the stage, this gallant gentleman takes an opportunity of mentioning to the audience, that he has been passing his time very agreeably." Mme De Staël's novel *Delphine* is treated a little more seriously as an immoral work. Smith ridicules the Romantic figure of the rebellious hero, oppressed by the narrowness of society and finding in violation of the laws and conventions of the world a kind of higher morality.

There exists, through the whole of this novel, a show of exquisite sensibility to the evils which individuals suffer by the inflexible rules of virtue prescribed by society, and an eager disposition to apologise for particular transgressions. . . .

Delphine is every where a great spirit, struggling with the shackles imposed upon her in common with the little world around her; and it is managed so, that her contempt of restrictions shall always appear to flow from the extent, variety, and splendour of her talents. The vulgarity of this heroism ought in some degree to diminish its value. Mr. Colquhoun, in his Police of the Metropolis, reckons up above 40,000 heroines of this species, most of whom, we dare to say, have at one time or another reasoned like the sentimental Delphine about the judgments of the world.

This is a comment on the Byronic hero (before he became the property of Byron) as effective, in its way, as the seduction scene in *Madame Bovary*, where Rodolphe's trite declarations of passion and higher morality are set against the background of a livestock exhibition.

Smith's insistence on a moral standard for literature, however, did not bring him into the camp of Sunday-school prudery. His views on preaching and associationistic philosophy led him to depend more on example than precept in teaching morality. He calls Hannah More's *Cœlebs in Search of a Wife* a "dramatic sermon" rather than a novel, because of its heavy-handed evangelical moralizing. One of the characters, acting as mouthpiece for Mrs. More, condemns the theater as immoral per se; and Smith, displaying his own notions of literary morality, remarks:

To behold the child and his mother—the noble and the poor artisan—the monarch and his subjects—all ages and all ranks convulsed with one common anguish, and, with loud sobs and cries, doing involuntary homage to the God that made their hearts! What wretched infatuation to interdict such amusements as these! What a blessing that mankind can be allured from sensual gratification, to find relaxation and pleasure in such pursuits! But the excellent Mr. Stanley is uniformly paltry and narrow—always trembling at the idea of being entertained, and thinking no Christian safe who is not dull.

By the same standards, he praises the morality of Thomas Hope's *Anastasius*, a novel abounding in seductions, bloodshed, and treachery, because it leaves the reader, "with a greater disgust at vice, and a more thorough conviction of the necessity of subjugating passion" simply by accurately portraying the evils of life.

Smith's third criterion for judging literature was mimetic. He praises Lister's *Granby* for presenting recognizable characters who were types of people met in society. His major objection to Mrs. More's *Cœlebs* is the absolute purity of its major characters, an objection made both on literary and on religious grounds. "Lucilla is totally uninteresting; so is Mr. Stanley; Dr. Barlow still worse; and Cœlebs a mere clod or dolt. Sir John and Lady Belfield are rather more interesting—and for a very obvious reason: they have some faults; they put us in mind of men and women;—they seem to belong to one common nature with ourselves."

The characters Smith thinks Mrs. More did best are Mrs.

Ranby, a self-righteous, overreligious prig, and her daughters, shallow and vapid flirts. In criticizing Lewis's *Alphonso*, Smith also finds a lack of mimetic accuracy in the portrayal of character and situation, and comments in a dry manner,

> We beg leave to submit to Mr. Lewis, if Alfonso, considering the great interest he has in the decision, might not interfere a little in the long argument carried on between Cæsario and Orsino, upon the propriety of putting him to death. To have expressed any decisive opinion upon the subject, might perhaps have been incorrect; but a few gentle hints as to that side of the question to which he leaned, might be fairly allowed to be no very unnatural incident.

Smith's use of the words "nature" and "unnatural" in the two passages just cited indicates the source of his esthetics. The empirical philosophy which dictated eighteenth-century thought and neo-classical standards in art was based on a view of "nature" as a set of universal, generalized laws of existence. Art had to imitate this "nature" by representing life and experience as they were most commonly apprehended by the human race. Smith's own lectures on moral philosophy insisted that beauty existed in a work of art when it faithfully represented some object, emotion, or action which was generally recognized as being beautiful in life.

Another neo-classical trait of Smith's criticism is his conviction that there is a fit and appropriate subject matter for literature, and that common or "low" experiences and characters are unsuitable for representation. In his correspondence with T. H. Lister, Smith insists that it would be disastrous to write a tragedy upon Perkin Warbeck, the unsuccessful false pretender to the throne of Henry VII, as no audience would accept as a tragic protagonist a low-born man who ended his life on a gibbet. In commenting on the same author's novel *Granby*, he disapproves of a depicted fistfight as another "low" topic. "Nobody should suffer his hero to have a black eye, or to be pulled by the nose. The Iliad would never have come down to these times if Agamemnon had given Achilles a box on the ear. We should have trembled for the Æneid, if any Tyrian nobleman had kicked the pious Æneas in the 4th book. Æneas may have deserved it; but he could not have founded the Roman Empire after so distressing an accident." By contrast, the passages he most admires in Lewis's *Alphonso* and Hope's *Anastasius* are those dealing with traditionally "high" subjects—warfare, royalty, and court intrigue.

III *Smith and the Romantics*

It seems obvious from Sydney Smith's literary canons that he was not a Romantic. His mimetic and didactic criteria for judging literature, his notions of "fit" subjects for poetry and drama, and his view of the artist as a craftsman whose task is to please the gentleman all mark his sensibility as belonging to the eighteenth, rather than to the nineteenth century. Even his own power of shrewd observation and witty commentary and his talent for satire are more appropriate to the age of Swift and Addison than to that of Lamb and De Quincey. Smith was not an anti-Romantic in the way that Jeffrey was, actively fighting the literary principles of Wordsworth and his followers; but he was a non-Romantic, neither by temperament nor by environment suited to the passions and ideas of the Romantics, and choosing to ignore rather than to fight them.

Interestingly enough, he was not as thoroughly cheerful as his good-humored writings would indicate; he was subject to fits of melancholia which suspiciously resemble the typically Romantic malady of ennui, or *Weltschmerz*. But rather than supposing this a natural result of a disordered world, as did Childe Harold or Werther or their creators, Smith struggled against what he considered an unnatural condition. His advice to a friend on combating low spirits shows in what an unromantic direction he thought health to lie.

Nobody has suffered more from low spirits than I have done—so I feel for you. 1st. Live as well as you dare. 2nd. Go into the shower-bath with a small quantity of water at a temperature low enough to give you a slight sensation of cold, 75° or 80°. 3rd. Amusing books. 4th. Short views of human life—not further than dinner or tea. 5th. Be as busy as you can. 6th. See as much as you can of those friends who respect and like you. 7th. And of those acquaintances who amuse you. 8th. Make no secret of low spirits to your friends, but talk of them freely—they are always worse for dignified concealment. 9th. Attend to the effects tea and coffee produce upon you. 10th. Compare your lot with that of other people. 11th. Don't expect too much from human life—a sorry business at the best. 12th. *Avoid poetry, dramatic representations (except comedy), music, serious novels, melancholy sentimental people, and everything likely to excite feeling or motion not ending in active benevolence.*[8]

Those aspects of Romanticism that lay outside of literature—religious enthusiasm, political egalitarianism, doctrines of human perfectibility—he opposed directly and vigorously in his essays on Methodism, politics, and the like. Another point upon which Smith's opinions differ markedly from those of the Romantics is in his view of primitive nations. Smith wrote more than thirty articles for the *Edinburgh* reviewing books of travels, more than he wrote on any other subject; and many of these articles deal with voyages to primitive lands and cultures. The Romantics tended to find in such cultures the Rousseauistic "noble savage," uncorrupted by civilization; Smith looked from a more rationalistic point of view at societies exhibiting earlier, and therefore inferior, stages of human progress than the societies of Europe. A typical essay of this sort deals with the Ashantee tribe of the Gold Coast of Africa and includes detailed analysis of such institutions as government, crafts, architecture, economy, and religious practices (including human sacrifice).[9]

Smith also uses books of travel for satire, employing outlandish features of an alien land to comment on life at home, in a manner less subtle and less contrived than that of *Gulliver's Travels,* but nevertheless reflective of Augustan wit. In a review of an account of South American fauna, Smith makes the following remarks:[10]

The campanero may be heard three miles!—this single little bird being more powerful than the belfry of a cathedral, ringing for a new dean, —just appointed on account of shabby politics, small understanding and good family! . . .

To what purpose, we say, is a bird placed in the woods of Cayenne, with a bill a yard long, making a noise like a puppy dog, and laying eggs in hollow trees? The toucans, to be sure, might retort, to what purpose were gentlemen in Bond Street created? To what purpose were certain foolish prating Members of Parliament created? . . .

There is no end of such questions. So we will not enter into the metaphysics of the toucan. . . .

The sloth, in its wild state, spends its life in trees, and never leaves them but from force or accident. . . . But what is most extraordinary, he lives not *upon* the branches, but under them. He moves suspended, rests suspended, sleeps suspended, and passes his life in suspense—like a young clergyman distantly related to a bishop.

CHAPTER 8

Style and the Man

I Smith and the Sesquipedalianists

"WHENEVER you have wrote any thing you think *particularly fine* said the old College tutor to his pupil—Scratch it out instantly." [1] This comment which Sydney Smith made in 1799, when he himself was a tutor and struggling with the turgid, over-elaborate prose of his pupil, is characteristic of his dislike for pedantic and ostentatious writing. His first article for the *Edinburgh Review* sharply criticizes Dr. Samuel Parr for thinking,

that eloquence consists not in an exuberance of beautiful images—not in simple and sublime conceptions—not in the feelings of the passions; but in a studious arrangement of *sonorous, exotic, and sesquipedal* words: a very ancient error, which corrupts the style of the young, and wearies the patience of sensible men. In some of his combinations of words the Doctor is singularly unhappy. We have the *din of superficial cavillers,* the *prancings of giddy ostentation, fluttering vanity, hissing scorn, dank cold,* &c. &c. &c.[2]

In the next issue, Smith takes an author to task for overusing the pedantic device of classical allusion. "The whole treatise is composed like a school-boy's theme, where the plainest thing that he states, must be illustrated with a simile; and he must also at every step undergo the labour of turning up his classical dictionary, to find out some virtuous Greek or Roman, who did something or other, which had either some or no resemblance to what he is writing about." [3]

Smith's own education, heavy in the classicism of Winchester and Oxford, made him a master of the elaborate sentence, the obscure word, and the classical quotation. On occasion he could use elaborate sentence structure for its authoritative effect, as in the *Peter Plymley Letters:*

If there were any great scenery, any heroic feelings, any blaze of ancient virtue, any exalted death, any termination of England that would be ever remembered, ever honoured in that western world, where liberty is now retiring, conquest would be more tolerable, and ruin more sweet; but it is doubly miserable to become slaves abroad, because we would be tyrants at home; to persecute, when we are contending against persecution; and to perish, because we have raised up worse enemies within, from our own bigotry, than we are exposed to without, from the unprincipled ambition of France.[4]

More typical elaborate sentences are the following, in which his intent is to undercut, rather than to inflate, both the style and the subject.

If a prudent man see a child playing with a porcelain cup of great value, he takes the vessel out of his hand, pats him on the head, tells him his mamma will be sorry if it is broken, and gently cheats him into the use of some less precious substitute. Why will Lord Sidmouth meddle with the Toleration Act, when there are so many other subjects in which his abilities might be so eminently useful—when enclosure bills are drawn up with such scandalous negligence—turnpike roads so shamefully neglected—and public conveyances illegitimately loaded in the face of day, and in defiance of the wisest legislative provisions?[5]

In a similar way, he frequently quotes lines of Latin and Greek verse in such inappropriate contexts that the ridicule is directed both against his subject and the pedantic practice itself. For example, in speaking of the penal colony at Botany Bay, Smith points out that stories of convicts making a great deal of money in Australia through land grants and speculations necessarily make transportation seem to the would-be thief more of an opportunity than a punishment. He then quotes Virgil's lines describing the pleading of dead souls for a passage across the Styx in Charon's boat: "Stabant orantes primi transmittere cursum,/ Tendebantque manus, ripæ ulterioris amore."[6]

Another device of pseudo-classical diction which Smith deplores and uses as a foil to his wit is the polished, but superfluous, epithet or the Latinate word coinage. He once parodied Pope in two couplets:

> Why has not man a collar and a log?
> For this plain reason—man is not a dog.

> Why is not man served up with sauce in dish?
> For this plain reason—man is not a fish.[7]

In his essays, he uses Popean epithets liberally and with tongue
in cheek. Members of Parliament who support the Game Laws
become "legislators of the trigger," and the governor of the infant
colony of Botany Bay is called the "Romulus of the South Pole."
Latinate neologisms are just as frequent. Dr. Parr's pedantic
praise of learning becomes "eulogomania"; children who eat fruit
are "frugivorous"; and preferences for rare or well-done roasts are
called "semisanguineous partiality" and "a taste for cinereous
and torrified meats." Occasionally Smith combines Latinity and
epithet, and an explorer from Yorkshire is translated into an
"Eboracic traveller."

Such wordplay is put to more polemic use when Smith ridicules
the cant of his own time rather than the neo-classical jargon of
the previous century. He picks up and ridicules such slogans as
"just and necessary war" and "the Church is in danger," used to
justify tyranny and persecution. He takes particular delight in
being able to use an opponent's own words against him. He points
out, for example, that many of the Vice Presidents of the Society
for the Suppression of Vice ride to the hounds; and after quoting,
from the Society's own papers, a description of bear-baiting as a
practice designed to "stimulate those animals [dogs and bears],
by means of the antipathies which Providence has thought proper
to place between them, to worry and tear, and often to destroy
each other," Smith remarks, "We take it for granted, that the
reader sees clearly that no part of this description can possibly
apply to the case of *hunting*." [8]

Sydney Smith's argumentative wit did not depend entirely on
his clever turns of phrase or exaggerated pedantries. He could
seize upon the weak spot in some victim's logic and ridicule it
with sly understatement, as, "An informer, whether he is paid by
the week, like the agents of this society—or by the crime, as in
common cases,—is, in general, a man of a very indifferent character," [9] or with flawlessly logical overstatement, as,

We observe that Mrs. More, in one part of her work, falls into the
common error about dress. . . .

"Oh! if women in general knew what was their real interest, if they could guess with what a charm even the *appearance* of modesty invests its possessor, they would dress decorously from mere self-love, if not from principle. The designing would assume modesty as an artifice; the coquet would adopt it as an allurement; . . . and the voluptuous as the most infallible art of seduction."

If there is any truth in this passage, nudity becomes a virtue; and no decent woman, for the future, can be seen in garments.[10]

Smith's gift for pertinent (and sometimes impertinent) analogy and his ability to shift swiftly from the particular to the general or vice versa gave him another weapon, the allegorical anecdote. His use of the metaphorical ship of state and the village of tyrants in the *Peter Plymley Letters* has already been noted.[11] In the *Letters to Archdeacon Singleton*, in protesting the way the bishops of the Ecclesiastical Commission have stripped the cathedrals of wealth and power in order to satisfy a popular demand for church reform, Smith invents an old Dutch Chronicle, containing a remarkably applicable passage. He goes on, in fifteenth-century language, to describe a great meeting of the clergy in the Bailiwick of Dort, in the course of which the bishops feed the dinner of the deans and canons to the poor and receive great praise for their generosity. He even appends a solemn and scholarly note to the apocryphal story, defining the *sleich* as "A measure in the Bailiwick of Dort, containing two gallons one pint English dry measure." [12]

II *Table-Talk*

As popular as his writings made him with the general public, it was his power as a conversationalist and table wit which was Smith's greatest asset in the social circles he frequented. Examples of his quick wit are numerous. He described Lady Cork as being "so moved by a charity sermon that she begged me to lend her a guinea for her contribution. I did so. She never repaid me, and spent it on herself." [13] The Prince of Wales's fantastic oriental pavilion at the sea looked to Smith as if "St. Paul's had come to Brighton and pupped." [14]

A rarer gift, perhaps, than wit, was his good humor. A sharp sally or striking *mot* may make the hearer smile (or perhaps wince) at its cleverness, but it is usually rooted in a cynical

[142]

rather than comic view of humanity. Smith's good-natured ability to grasp the essential ludicrousness behind every human situation and to build up a series of comical images can be only partially reported or even described. Thomas Moore tells in his diary of a breakfast at Samuel Rogers'. "Smith full of comicality and fancy; kept us all in roars of laughter. In talking of the stories about dram-drinkers catching fire, pursued the idea in every possible shape. The inconvenience of a man coming too near the candle when he was speaking, 'Sir, your observation has caught fire.' Then imagined a parson breaking into a blaze in the pulpit; the engines called to put him out; no water to be had, the man at the waterworks being an Unitarian or an atheist." [15]

Georgian wit was frequently coarse, even in mixed company, and cruel. Lord Palmerston's notebooks record many samples of very low and blunt humor, for example, "Lady Townshend hearing of some certain young ladies who were very ready to oblige their friends with certain manual operations, said she supposed they thought a bird in the hand worth two in the bush." [16] And John Hookham Frere, during the reigns of Scott and Byron as the literary lions of society, observed that "Great poets formerly (Homer and Milton) were blind; now they are lame." [17] Smith's writings naturally reflect in part the taste of his own day; his comparison between ridiculing Methodists and exterminating lice, his droll description of the effects on Napoleon's army of the English embargo upon bark and rhubarb, and the personal nature of his political attacks on Spencer Perceval and George Canning are in questionable taste by modern standards.

Yet, the best known and most quoted wit of his time, he was also among the least offensive to taste and sensibility. Samuel Rogers, himself noted for an acid tongue, remarked soon after Smith's death that Smith's idea of propriety had kept him from the full exercise of his powers as a humorist;[18] and Lord Dudley, whose absent-mindedness and eventual periods of insanity made him a natural target for jokes, once remarked to Smith, "You have been laughing at me constantly, Sydney, for the last seven years, and yet in all that time you never said a single thing to me that I wished unsaid." [19] Macaulay tells of a dinner at which Smith and the caustic Rogers were present; the two wits divided, rather than shared, the conversation, speaking only one at a time. "The one who had possession of the company was always Sydney Smith," says Macaulay, "and the one who was silent was always Rogers." [20]

III *The Teacher of the People*

A French critic, writing at the end of the nineteenth century, said of Sydney Smith, "Strictly speaking, Sydney Smith is not a man of letters. He can only be regarded as a middle-class Englishman who, in traditional fashion, speaks out his mind on public affairs, writes in periodicals to complain when he feels himself injured by some law or some official, and often takes the floor at meetings." [21] If the phrase "man of letters" is to be taken to mean a practitioner of belles-lettres, the comment is just. Smith wrote very little literary criticism and no fiction, drama, or poetry. However, if continued interest in his writings is to be any measure of a man's literary importance, then Sydney Smith is a man of letters. His collected works went through four editions from 1839 to 1848; and, between 1858 and 1956, seven different editions of selected writings were published in England and America.

At the bottom of this persistent popularity is, of course, Smith's wit. His ability to amuse successive generations of readers must be given major credit for his reputation. Yet it is not only that he makes people laugh but that he makes them laugh at something —hypocrisy, cant, pomposity, self-interest—the eternal follies of social and political officialdom. His rank in life, allowing him to see society from top to bottom, made him an informed and keen observer of his times, much like Chaucer. And, like Chaucer, he lived at a time when English society was vigorous, earthy, and in a period of transition. Removed by one generation from the trade of his family's past and by one generation from the aristocracy of its future, Smith is placed firmly in the liberal middle class which first came to significant political power in Britain during his lifetime and dominated all of Western civilization within the century. His practical views on morality, justice, toleration, education, and social reform foreshadowed middle-class opinions and to a great extent formed them; for the *Edinburgh Review*, like its founder, crossed social boundaries, spoke on all subjects to all kinds of people, and provided a voice for the opinions of the new ruling class.

[144]

Sydney Smith's reputation reached its height at the same time that middle-class power reached its height, toward the end of the nineteenth century. His writings were judged less for their pure humor than for the views they expressed. Sir Leslie Stephen, writing in the *Cornhill Magazine*, said, "In a London party he might throw the reins upon the neck of his fancy and go on playing with a ludicrous image. . . . In his writings he aims almost as straight at his mark as Swift, and is never diverted by the spirit of pure fun. The humour always illuminates well-strung logic." [22] George Saintsbury, a follower of Matthew Arnold in attacking middle-class values, considered Smith the most original and interesting of the early *Edinburgh* reviewers and found the sure touch of his wit similar to Voltaire's; but at the same time Saintsbury condemned Smith's point of view as representative of the bourgeois Philistinism that had made Victorian art and culture second-rate and shoddy.[23]

In distinguishing Smith from others who had fought for the same causes, his daughter said, "I think he has one peculiarity above almost any writer of his day—that of *attracting public attention*—he was born for a *teacher* of the people." [24] Teaching, perhaps, is the best description of what Sydney Smith actually did. Through lessons on particular issues, from toleration to game laws, Smith expounded the liberal point of view. His faith in rational argument and distrust of dogma, his religious latitudinarianism, his concern for individual injustices, his scepticism about the innate value of established institutions—all are characteristic of liberal thought.

In view of the reassessment which liberalism is undergoing these days, both by its opponents and by its adherents, a renewed interest in Sydney Smith seems in order. The liberal Whig tradition to which Smith belonged has, since his time, shifted its economic base from the sanctity of private property and laissez faire to leveling taxation and the welfare state; but otherwise it has come down to us more or less intact. Smith's thought exemplifies liberalism at its best, in the value it places on the liberty and potentiality of the individual, and at its worst, in its increasing rejection of humanism for scientism in guiding the affairs of mankind. Interestingly, he does not exemplify liberalism at its weakest, in its passionate faith in the wisdom and virtue of the common man—his sense of humor could never allow this. Perhaps the most valuable aspect of Smith's liberalism is this sense of humor. Modern liberalism does not depend upon a philosophy but on a point of view. It has neither the left's coldly empirical materialism nor the right's absolute acceptance of a priori judgments. Instead, liberalism is based on the notion of a world in flux, where absolutes are difficult, if not impossible, to determine, and decisions can only be relatively effective in any given situation. Its continuing validity as a way of life depends on its capacity for constant readjustment, its willingness to re-examine today what it said yesterday and to discard tomorrow what it does today. If liberalism takes itself too seriously and allows the opinions of the moment to harden into dogma, it destroys its own foundation.

That is why the liberal cannot afford to lose his sense of humor. In order to function in a world of constantly shifting dogmas, creeds, and ideologies, he must retain the capacity to recognize the essential ludicrousness implicit in all human action. And here he can still learn from the keen eye and sharp tongue of Sydney Smith.

Notes and References

Chapter One

1. "Public Schools," *Works of the Rev. Sydney Smith,* 4th ed. (London, 1848), I, 391. Essays cited from the *Works* will be cross-referenced for their original appearance in the *Edinburgh Review* according to volume, number, and article number in the review. This article is *ER,* XVI, xxxii (1810), Art. 3.

2. G. C. Heseltine, "Five Letters of Sydney Smith," *London Mercury,* XXI (1930), 516.

3. Catherine Amelia Smith, "Narrative for my grandchildren," unpub. ms. in the possession of Mr. David Holland, p. 26.

4. Mrs. William [Susan Emily] Hicks Beach, *A Cotswold Family: Hicks and Hicks Beach* (London, 1909), pp. 307–13.

5. Lady Holland, *A Memoir of the Reverend Sydney Smith* (New York, 1855), I, 233. The authoress, Sydney Smith's daughter Saba, became Lady Holland when her husband, the famous physician, was created Sir Henry Holland, Bart. She will be referred to in both text and notes as Saba Holland in order to avoid confusing her with Elizabeth, Lady Holland, wife of the third Baron Holland, and Smith's lifelong friend.

6. Morchard Bishop, ed., *Recollections of the Table-Talk of Samuel Rogers* (London, 1952), pp. 151–52.

7. "The Rev. Sydney Smith," *Monographs: Personal and Social* (New York, 1873), p. 255.

8. *Works,* I, iii.

9. For a detailed account of all evidence on the founding of the *Edinburgh Review* see John L. Clive, *Scotch Reviewers: The Edinburgh Review 1802–1815* (Cambridge, Mass., 1957), pp. 186–97.

10. *The Life and Times of Henry, Lord Brougham* (New York, 1871), I, 176–81.

11. Arthur Aspinall, *Politics and the Press: c. 1780–1850* (London, 1949), pp. 285–86.

12. *ER,* II, iii (1803), 268

13. [Isaac D'Israeli,] *Flim-Flams! or the Life and Errors of My*

[147]

Uncle and His Friends by Messieurs Tag, Rag, and Bobtail (London, 1806), III, 41.

14. *The Poetical Works of Sir Alexander Boswell,* ed. Robert Howie Smith (Glasgow, 1871), pp. 129–30.

15. Leonard Horner, ed., *Memoirs and Correspondence of Francis Horner, M. P.* (Boston, 1853), I, 219–21.

16. Nowell C. Smith, ed., *The Letters of Sydney Smith* (Oxford, 1953), I, 79.

17. [Henry Thomas,] Lord Cockburn, *Life of Lord Jeffrey with a Selection from his Correspondence* (Philadelphia, 1856), II, 63–65.

18. Brougham, *Life and Times,* I, 185.

19. John Gibson Lockhart, *Memoirs of the Life of Sir Walter Scott, Bart.* (Boston, 1861), III, 16.

20. Cockburn, *Jeffrey,* I, 232; Smith, *Works,* I, iv; Brougham, *Life and Times,* I, 180–81.

Chapter Two

1. Richard Pares, *King George III and the Politicians* (Oxford, 1953), p. 24.

2. John Ashton, *The Dawn of the XIXth Century in England* (London, 1896), pp. 177–78.

3. *Works,* I, 100–04; *ER,* II, iii (1803), Art. 22. A second article on the same topic, *ER,* V, x (1805), Art. 3, may have been written by Smith.

4. *Works,* III, 309–94.

5. *Ibid.,* p. 315.

6. *Ibid.,* p. 353.

7. "Letter on the Curates' Salary Bill," *Works,* I, 252–64; *ER,* XIII, xxv (1808), Art. 2. See also *Letters,* I, 136–37.

8. *Letters,* I, 97.

9. *Works,* II, 270–91; *ER,* XXXVII, lxxiv (1822), Art. 7.

10. *Works,* III, 366.

11. *Ibid.,* pp. 363–65.

12. *Ibid.,* p. 370.

13. *Ibid.,* p. 355.

14. *Letters,* II, 664.

15. *Elizabeth, Lady Holland to Her Son: 1821–1845,* ed. Earl of Ilchester (London, 1946), p. 167.

16. *Letters,* II, 596.

17. Sir George Otto Trevelyan, *The Life and Letters of Lord Macaulay,* World's Classics ed. (London, 1932), I, 212. Daniel Wilson was Bishop of Calcutta.

18. *Letters,* II, 707.

19. "On Toleration," *Miscellaneous Sermons* (Philadelphia, 1846), p. 216. Unless otherwise stated, Smith's sermons will be cited from this volume.

20. Saba Holland, *Memoir*, I, 57–58.

21. *Letters*, II, 654.

22. Saba Holland, *Memoir*, I, 48–49.

23. "On Good Friday," p. 79.

24. "A Sermon on the Rules of Christian Charity," *Works*, III, 275–91.

25. *Works*, III, 157–66.

26. *Ibid.*, pp. 293–304.

27. "On the Importance of Public Worship," p. 46.

28. "On Temptation," p. 186.

29. "On Repentance," pp. 14–15.

30. Saba Holland, *Memoir*, I, 48–50.

31. "On the Importance of Public Worship," p. 43.

32. "Upon the Best Mode of Charity," p. 121.

33. "Dr. Rennel," *Works*, I, 10; *ER*, I, i (1802), Art. 9.

34. "Archdeacon Nares," *Works*, I, 29; *ER*, I, i (1802), Art. 20.

35. "Proceedings of the Society for the Suppression of Vice," *Works*, I, 273–86; *ER*, XIII, xxvi (1809), Art. 4.

36. *ER*, XLIV, lxxxviii (1826), Art. 7.

37. *ER*, III, v (1803), Art. 8.

38. "Memoirs of Sydney Smith," *Eclectic Review*, CII (1855), 191.

39. "Sydney Smith as a Minister of Religion," *Princeton Review*, XXVIII (1856), 421.

40. "Sydney Smith's Life and Works," *Christian Observer*, XXX (1855), 258–59.

41. G. F. A. Best, "The Whigs and the Church Establishment in the Age of Grey and Holland," *History*, XLV (1960), 104.

42. Donald Southgate, *The Passing of the Whigs: 1832–1886* (London and New York, 1962), p. 218.

43. "Upon the Best Mode of Charity," p. 119.

Chapter Three

1. Saba Holland, *Memoir*, I, 91.

2. "On Toleration," pp. 215–22.

3. "Parnell and Ireland," *Works*, I, 167–75; *ER*, X, xx (1807), Art. 4.

4. "Preface," *Works*, I, v.

5. *Works*, III, 87.

6. *Ibid.*, pp. 136–37.

7. *Ibid.*, p. 114.

8. *Ibid.*, p. 85.

9. *Ibid.*, pp. 80–81.

10. *Ibid.*, p. 106.

11. *Ibid.*, pp. 127–28.

12. *Ibid.*, p. 61.

13. "Catholic Question," *Works*, III, 55; *ER*, XLV, xc (1827), Art. 7.

14. *ER*, XIII, xxv (1808), Art. 5; XIV, xxvii (1809), Art. 5; XX, xxxix (1812), Art. 4; XXI, xli (1813), Art. 4; XXXIV, lxvii (1820), Art. 2; XLI, lxxxi (1824), Art. 7; and XLV, xc (1827), Art. 7. All but the second and third, on the appointment of bishops and the Duke of Sussex' speech, are reprinted in *Works*.

15. *Works*, III, 183–203, 237–91.

16. "Fragment on the Irish Roman Catholic Church," *Works*, III, 485–501.

17. *Memoirs, Journal and Correspondence of Thomas Moore*, ed. Lord John Russell (London, 1853), VII, 51.

18. "Methodism," *Works*, I, 183; *ER*, XI, xxii (1808), Art. 5.

19. *Letters*, I, 131.

20. *Ibid.*, pp. 113–17.

21. "Indian Missions," *Works*, I, 212–51; *ER*, XII, xxiii (1808), Art. 9.

22. "Review of Sydney Smith's Sermons," *Christian Observer*, VIII (1809), 578–98.

23. "Methodism," *Works*, I, 287–301; *ER*, XIV, xxvii (1809), Art. 3.

24. "Toleration," *Works*, I, 414–25; *ER*, XVII, xxxiv (1811), Art. 8; and "Protestant Dissenters," *ER*, XIX, xxxvii (1811), Art. 6. The Test and Corporation Acts were finally done away with in 1828.

25. "Dissenters' Marriages," *ER*, XXXV, lxix (1821), 63. The Dissenter Marriage Bill, recognizing non-Anglican marriages, passed in 1836.

Chapter Four

1. Heseltine, "Five Letters," p. 513.

2. *Letters*, I, 247–48.

3. *Memoirs of Horner*, I, 295.

4. *Letters*, II, 782.

5. *Elementary Sketches of Moral Philosophy* (London, 1850), p. 291.

6. *Ibid.*, p. 3.

7. *Ibid.*, p. 158.

8. *Ibid.*, p. 171.

9. *Ibid.*, p. 111.

10. *Ibid.*, p. 267.
11. *Ibid.*, p. 376.
12. *Ibid.*, p. 123.
13. *Works*, III, 74.
14. *Moral Phil.*, pp. 135–45.
15. "Speech at Taunton," *Works*, III, 218–19.
16. *Moral Phil.*, pp. 125, 139.
17. *Ibid.*, p. 179.
18. Saba Holland, *Memoir*, I, 240.
19. *Letters*, I, 400–01; II, 769.
20. *Moral Phil.*, p. 364.
21. "Dr. Parr," *Works*, I, 1–9; *ER*, I, i (1802), Art. 2.
22. "Godwin's Reply to Parr," *ER*, I, i (1802), Art. 3.
23. Southgate, *Passing of the Whigs*, p. 21.
24. "Bentham on Fallacies," *Works*, II, 387–415; *ER*, XLII, lxxxiv (1825), Art. 4.
25. G. M. Trevelyan, *Lord Grey of the Reform Bill*, 2nd ed. (London *et al.*, 1929), p. 317.
26. "Ballot," *Works*, III, 417–42.
27. "Dr. Rennel," *Works*, I, 15; *ER*, I, i (1802), Art. 9.
28. "Necker's Last Views," *Works*, I, 53; *ER*, I, ii (1803), Art. 10.
29. "John Bowles," *Works*, I, 20–24; *ER*, I, i (1802), Art. 12.
30. *ER*, XIII, xxv (1808), Art. 14. Written by Jeffrey, this article was for a long time attributed to Brougham.
31. *QR*, I (1809), 193–226. For a list of Southey's contributions to the *Quarterly*, see *The Life and Correspondence of Robert Southey*, ed. Rev. Charles Cuthbert Southey (London, 1850), VI, 400–01. For Southey's animosity toward Smith and the *Edinburgh* as a motive for his reviews, see Geoffrey Carnall, *Robert Southey and His Age* (Oxford, 1960), pp. 99, 130, 135.
32. "Sydney Smith's Sermons," *QR*, I (1809), 387–98; "Sydney Smith's Visitation Sermon," *QR*, III (1810), 185–94. *Poole's Index* identifies Croker as the author of both articles.
33. "Rose's Observations on Fox," *Works*, I, 319–44; *ER*, XIV, xxvii (1809), Art. 13.
34. "Characters of Mr. Fox," *Works*, I, 310–18; *ER*, XIV, xxvii (1809), Art. 5.
35. "Heywood's Vindication of Mr. Fox's History," *Works*, I, 426–48; *ER*, XVIII, xxxvi (1811), Art. 3.
36. Cockburn, *Jeffrey*, II, 105.
37. "Mr. Canning's Letters to Earl Camden," *QR*, II (1809), 412–26. The issue is dated November, a month before Jeffrey's letter, but

it was not unusual for either the *Quarterly* or the *Edinburgh* to come out a month or two late without changing the nominal publication date.

38. *ER*, XV, xxx (1810), Art. 15. Canning's *Letter* is listed in the same issue among new publications (p. 529), but it is not reviewed.

39. *Letters*, I, 186.

40. Cockburn, *Jeffrey*, II, 106. Jeffrey is alluding to the battle between Sir Francis Burdett and the House of Commons on the question of the "privilege of the House," which resulted in Burdett's imprisonment and popular uprisings throughout the country, but which never reached the proportions of a civil war. It was, in justice to Jeffrey, a surprising and alarming display of Radical popularity and strength.

41. "Walcheren Expedition," *ER*, XVII, xxxiv (1811), Art. 4.

42. "Papers relative to the Negociations of the Marquis Wellesley and the Earl of Moira, for forming a New Administration," *Annual Register*, LIV (1812), 360–68. See also Michael Roberts, "The Ministerial Crisis of May–June 1812," *English Historical Review*, LI (1936), 466–87.

43. "Negotiations for a Ministry," *ER*, XX, xxxix (1812), Art. 2.

Chapter Five

1. "Trimmer and Lancaster," *Works*, I, 157–66; *ER*, IX, xvii (1806), Art. 12.

2. "Lancaster's Improvements in Education," *ER*, XI, xxi (1807), Art. 4.

3. *Letters*, I, 219.

4. "Professional Education," *Works*, I, 345–61; *ER*, XV, xxix (1809), Art. 3.

5. "Calumnies against Oxford," *ER*, XVI, xxxi (1810), Art. 7. Smith wrote pp. 177–87; the rest was by Playfair and Knight.

6. "Public Schools," *Works*, I, 383–93; *ER*, XVI, xxxii (1810), Art. 3.

7. "Hamilton's Method of Teaching Languages," *Works*, II, 453–80; *ER*, XLIV, lxxxvii (1826), Art. 2.

8. "Female Education," *Works*, I, 362–82; *ER*, XV, xxx (1810), Art. 3.

9. Saba Holland, *Memoir*, I, 146.

10. *Letters*, I, 293.

11. "Speech on the Reform Bill," *Works*, III, 223.

12. "Game Laws," *Works*, II, 35–52; *ER*, XXXI, lxii (1819), Art. 2.

13. "Spring Guns," *Works*, II, 181–95; *ER*, XXXV, lxix (1821), Art. 7. See also "Man Traps and Spring Guns," *Works*, II, 216–31; *ER*, XXXV, lxx (1821), Art. 8.

14. "Game Laws," *Works,* II, 318–32; *ER,* XXXIX, lxxvii (1823), Art. 2.
15. *Memoirs of the Life of Elizabeth Fry* [ed. K. Fry and R. E. Cresswell] (London, 1847), II, 310.
16. "State of Prisons," *Works,* II, 196–215; *ER,* XXXV, lxx (1821), Art. 2.
17. *Letters,* I, 326.
18. "Prisons," *Works,* II, 244–69; *ER,* XXXVI, lxxii (1822), Art. 3.
19. "Botany Bay," *Works,* II, 303–4; *ER,* XXXVIII, lxxv (1823), Art. 4.
20. "Cruel Treatment of Untried Prisoners," *Works,* II, 333–52; *ER,* XXXIX, lxxviii (1824), Art. 2.
21. "Counsel for Prisoners," *Works,* III, 1–27; *ER,* LXV, lxxxix (1826), Art. 3.
22. "Mad Quakers," *Works,* I, 468–79; *ER,* XXIII, xlv (1814), Art. 8. A subsequent article, *ER,* XXVIII, lvi (1817), Art. 8, surveying the deplorable conditions in most insane asylums, may also be Smith's.
23. "Vaccination and Small-Pox," *ER,* XXXVII, lxxiv (1822), Art. 2.
24. "Chimney Sweepers," *Works,* II, 79–93; *ER,* XXXII, lxiv (1819), Art. 3.
25. "Poor-Laws," *Works,* II, 121–43; *ER,* XXXIII, lxv (1820), Art. 5; and "Scarlett's Poor-Bill," *Works,* II, 232–43; *ER,* XXXVI, lxxi (1821), Art. 6.
26. *Works,* II, 143.
27. Saba Holland, *Memoir,* I, 296.

Chapter Six

1. *Letters,* I, 305.
2. Henry Richard Vassal [Fox], Third Lord Holland, *Further Memoirs of the Whig Party 1807–1821 with some Miscellaneous Reminiscences* (New York, 1905), p. 63n.
3. *QR,* XXI (1819), 124ff.
4. *Letters,* I, 312.
5. "America," *Works,* II, 13–34; *ER,* XXXI, lxi (1818), Art. 6.
6. "America," *Works,* II, 107–20; *ER,* XXXIII, lxv (1820), Art. 3.
7. "America," *Works,* II, 353–72; *ER,* XL, lxxx (1824), Art. 7.
8. *Letters,* I, 271.
9. "Barlow's Columbiad," *ER,* XV, xxix (1809), Art. 2.
10. Cockburn, *Jeffrey,* II, 121.
11. *Letters,* I, 386. In the letter to Jeffrey, Smith refers to a "Miss Wright" as the author he had been reviewing. This was probably Fanny Wright (Mme Frances D'Arusmont), who was born in Scotland, married a Frenchman, and, after separating from her husband,

lectured and wrote in the United States. Her tragedy, *Altorf,* was
published in 1819, and was probably the work under consideration.

12. "J. G. C. Brainard," in *The Shock of Recognition,* ed. Edmund
Wilson, 2nd. ed. (New York, 1955), pp. 85–86.

13. *Poetical Works of William Wordsworth* (Oxford, 1958), IV,
132.

14. "Letters on American Debts," *Works,* III, 465–77.

15. Literally, "On the Greek Kalends." Since the Greeks used no
Kalends in reckoning time, this proverbially means "Never."

16. *Letters,* II, 813.

17. Saba Holland, *Memoir,* I, 358.

18. *Ibid.,* pp. 264–68.

19. "Sydney Smith's Works," *North American Review,* LIX (1844),
05–6.

20. "Sydney Smith," *North American Review,* LXXXII (1856), 108.

21. "Sydney Smith," *Democratic Review,* XIV (1844), 567.

22. William Kirkland, "Character and Opinions of the Late Rev.
Sydney Smith," *Godey's Ladies Book,* XXXIII (1846), 39.

23. "Sydney Smith," *Church Review,* IX (1856), 20.

24. "Sydney Smith as a Minister of Religion," *Princeton Review,*
XXVII (18 3), 418–43.

25. "Sy ney Smith," *Nation,* XXII (1876), 164.

26. Pa Mowbray Wheeler, *America Through British Eyes: A Study
of the A itude of* The Edinburgh Review *towards the United States
from 18 until 1861* (Rock Hill, S. C., 1935), p. 38.

27. Australia," *Works,* I, 56–71; *ER,* II, iii (1803), Art. 2.

28. Botany Bay," *Works,* II, 53–78; *ER,* XXXII, lxiii (1819), Art. 2.

29 'Botany Bay," *Works,* II, 292–317; *ER,* XXXVIII, lxxv, (1823),
Art.

Works, II, 360n. Italics mine.

Chapter Seven

1. "Matthew Lewis," *Works,* I, 32–36; *ER,* I, ii (1803), Art. 6.
Delphine," *Works,* I, 93–99; *ER,* II, iii (1803), Art. 17. "Hannah
More," *Works,* I, 302–9; *ER,* XIV, xxvii (1809), Art. 11. "Anastasius,"
Works, II, 168–80; *ER,* XXXV, lxix (1821), Art. 5. "Granby," *Works,*
II, 438–52; *ER,* XLIII, lxxxvi (1826), Art. 7.

2. *Letters,* I, 328, 342, 350–51, 373, 384–85, 389, 394, 404–5.

3. *Ibid.,* II, 504–11.

4. *Ibid.,* I, 250.

5. *Ibid.,* p. 281.

6. "Letters from a Mahratta Camp," *Works,* I, 462; *ER,* XXII, xliii
(1813), Art. 4.

7. "Sydney Smith," *Monographs*, p. 260.

8. *Letters*, I, 347–48. Italics mine.

9. "Mission to Ashantee," *Works*, II, 94–106; *ER*, XXXII, lxiv (1819), Art. 6.

10. "Waterton," *Works*, II, 416–37; *ER*, XLIII, lxxxvi (1826), Art. 2.

Chapter Eight

1. Heslington, "Five Letters," p. 514.

2. "Dr. Parr," *Works*, I, 6; *ER*, I, i (1802), Art. 2.

3. "Mad. Necker Réflexions sur le Divorce," *ER*, I, ii (1803), 68.

4. *Works*, III, 79.

5. "Toleration," *Works*, I, 414; *ER*, XVII, xxxiv (1811), Art. 8. Lord Sidmouth was Home Secretary in the Liverpool government.

6. "Botany Bay," *Works*, II, 315; *ER*, XXXVIII, lxxv (1823), Art. 4. The lines quoted are from the *Aeneid*, VI, 313–14. "They stand, pleading to be taken first, and stretch out their hands in longing for the distant shore."

7. Saba Holland, *Memoir*, I, 331.

8. "Society for the Suppression of Vice," *Works*, I, 282; *ER*, XIII, xxvi (1809), Art. 4.

9. *Ibid.*, p. 273.

10. "Hannah More," *Works*, I, 307; *ER*, XIV, xxvii (1809), Art. 11.

11. See above, pp. 62–63.

12. *Works*, III, 335–36.

13. *Table-Talk of Rogers*, p. 235.

14. E. Beresford Chancellor, *Life in Regency and Early Victorian Times* (New York and London, n.d.), p. 115.

15. *Memoirs of Moore*, V, 75.

16. Brian Connell, ed., *Portrait of a Golden Age: Intimate Papers of the Second Viscount Palmerston* (Boston, 1958), p. 69.

17. *Table-Talk of Rogers*, p. 139.

18. *Diary, Reminiscences, and Correspondence of Henry Crabb Robinson*, ed. Thomas Sadler (London and New York, 1872), II, 265.

19. Saba Holland, *Memoir*, I, 322.

20. Trevelyan, *Macaulay*, II, 62.

21. A. Chevrillon, *Sydney Smith et la Renaissance des Idées libérales en Angleterre au XIXᵉ siècle* (Paris, 1894), p. 243.

22. "Hours in a Library: The First Edinburgh Reviewers," *Cornhill*, XXXVIII (1878), 231.

23. "Sydney Smith," *Living Age*, CLXXVII (1888), 780–90; reprinted from *Macmillan's*, LVII.

24. Saba Holland, *Memoir*, I, 41.

Selected Bibliography

I. PRIMARY SOURCES

1. *Collected Works*

The Works of the Rev. Sydney Smith. 4 Vols. London: Longman,
Orne, Brown, Green, and Longmans, 1839–1840. The most inclusive of several later editions is the 4th. ed., London: Longmans, 1848; Philadelphia, Carey and Hart, 1848. It contains sixty-
five *Edinburgh Review* articles, a few otherwise unpublished
papers, and the following pamphlets which I have listed with
their original titles and dates of publication.

*Letters of Peter Plymley to my Brother Abraham who lives in the
Country.* London: J. Budd, 1807–1808.
The Lawyer that Tempted Christ. A Sermon. York: [privately printed],
1824.
Catholic Claims. A Speech. London: A. Cuddon, 1825.
A Sermon on Religious Charity. York: T. Wilson, 1825.
A Letter to the Electors, Upon the Catholic Question. York: T. Wilson,
1826.
Mr. Dyson's Speech to the Freeholders on Reform. London: J. Ridg-
way, 1831.
Speech at the Taunton Reform Meeting. London: [n.p.], 1831.
The New Reign. The Duties of Queen Victoria. A Sermon. London:
[n.p.], 1837.
A Letter to Archdeacon Singleton, on the Ecclesiastical Commission.
London: Longmans, 1837.
A Letter to Lord John Russell on the Church Bills. London: J. Mitchell,
1838.
Second Letter to Archdeacon Singleton. London: Longmans, 1838.
Third Letter to Archdeacon Singleton. London: Longmans, 1839.
Ballot. London: Longmans, 1839.
Letters on American Debts. London: Longman, Brown, Green, and
Longmans, 1843.
A Fragment on the Irish Roman Catholic Church. London: Longmans,
1845.

2. Collected Sermons

Sermons at St. Paul's, The Foundling Hospital, and Several Churches in London. London: Longmans, 1846.

Miscellaneous Sermons. Philadelphia: Carey and Hart, 1846. This volume includes the following earlier collections:

Six Sermons, preached in Charlotte Chapel. Edinburgh: [n.p.], 1800. Also in 2 vols., London: Longmans, 1801.

A Sermon upon the Conduct to be Observed by the Established Church towards Catholics and other Dissenters. London: [n.p.], 1807.

Sermons by the Rev. Sydney Smith. 2 vols. London: Cadell and Davies, 1809.

3. Uncollected Writings

Sermon preached before his Grace the Archbishop of York, and the Clergy of Malton, at the Visitation, August 1809. London: Carpenter, 1809.

Elementary Sketches of Moral Philosophy. London: Longman, Brown, Green, and Longmans, 1850.

The following *Edinburgh Review* articles were not included in Smith's *Works.* Those of disputed or doubtful authorship are marked with an asterisk (*). For evidences of authorship, see my article, "Sydney Smith in the *Edinburgh Review:* A New List," *Bulletin of the New York Public Library,* LXVI (1962), 589–602.

"Godwin's Reply to Parr," *ER,* I, i (1802), Art. 3.

* "Olivier's Travels in the Ottoman Empire, Egypt, and Persia," *ER,* I, i (1802), Art. 5.

* "Baldwin's Political Reflections Relative to Egypt," *ER,* I, i (1802), Art. 6.

* "Voyages dans . . . la France . . . ," *ER,* I, i (1802), Art. 10.

* "Acerbi's Travels through Sweden, &c.," *ER,* I, i (1802), Art. 24.

* "Sonnini's Travels in Greece and Turkey," *ER,* I, ii (1803), Art. 2.

* "Storch's Picture of Petersburgh," *ER,* I, ii (1803), Art. 4.

"Mad. Necker Réflexions sur le Divorce," *ER,* I, ii (1803), Art. 22.

"Accounts of the Egyptian Expedition," *ER,* II, iii (1803), Art. 4.

* "Ritson on Abstinence from Animal Food," *ER,* II, iii (1803), Art. 13.

* "Dr. Craven's Discourses," *ER,* II, iv (1803), Art. 14.

"Jacques Necker Cours de Morale Religieuse," *ER,* III, v (1803), Art. 8.

"Pallas's Travels in the Russian Empire," *ER,* III, v (1803), Art. 12.

"Voyage en Islande," *ER,* III, vi (1804), Art. 7.

* "Observations on Residence of the Clergy," *ER,* V, x (1805), Art. 3.

Selected Bibliography

"Lancaster's Improvement in Education," *ER*, XI, xxi (1807), Art. 4.

"Cordiner's Account of Ceylon," *ER*, XII, xxiii (1808), Art. 5.

"Dr. Milner and others on the Catholics of Ireland," *ER*, XIV, xxvii (1809), Art. 5.

"Calumnies Against Oxford," *ER*, XVI, xxxi (1810), Art. 7. Smith wrote pp. 177–87 of this review.

"Walcheren Expedition," *ER*, XVII, xxxiv (1811), Art. 4.

"Walton's Hispaniola," *ER*, XVII, xxxiv (1811), Art. 6.

"Kirkpatrick's Account of Nepaul," *ER*, XVIII, xxxvi (1811), Art. 8.

"Protestant Dissenters," *ER*, XIX, xxxvii (1811), Art. 6.

* "Negotiations for a Ministry," *ER*, XX, xxxix (1812), Art. 2.

"Duke of Sussex on Catholic Question," *ER*, XX, xxxix (1812), Art. 4.

"Mawe's Travels into the Interior of Brazil," *ER*, XX, xl (1812), Art. 3.

* "Lunatic Asylums," *ER*, XXVIII, lvi (1817), Art. 8.

"The Abbé Georgel," *ER*, XXX, lx (1818), Art. 7.

"Heude's Voyage and Travels," *ER*, XXXII, lxiii (1819), Art. 6.

"Burckhardt's Travels in Nubia," *ER*, XXXIV, lxvii (1820), Art. 5.

"Oxley's Tour in Botany Bay," *ER*, XXXIV, lxviii (1820), Art. 8.

"Dissenters' Marriages," *ER*, XXXV, lxix (1821), Art. 3.

* "Craven's Tour in South Italy," *ER*, XXXVI, lxxi (1821), Art. 8.

"Vaccination and Small-Pox," *ER*, XXXVII, lxxiv (1822), Art. 2.

"Captain Hall's Journal," *ER*, XL, lxxix (1824), Art. 2.

"Licensing of Alehouses," *ER*, XLIV, lxxxviii (1826), Art. 7.

"New South Wales," *ER*, XLVII, xciii (1828), Art. 4.

4. *Letters*

The Letters of Sydney Smith, ed. Nowell C. Smith. 2 vols. Oxford: The Clarendon Press, 1953. A number of Smith's letters, not included in this edition, may be found in the following places:

Dilworth, Ernest. "Letters of Sydney Smith," *Notes and Queries*, New Series, XI (1964), 419–21.

Green, David B. "Letters to Samuel Rogers from Tom Moore and Sydney Smith," *Notes and Queries*, New Series, II (1955), 542–43.

Heseltine, G. C. "Five Letters of Sydney Smith," *London Mercury*, XXI (1930), 512–17.

Hicks Beach, Mrs. William [Susan Emily]. *A Cotswold Family: Hicks and Hicks Beach*. London: Heinemann, 1909. Pp. 307–35.

Lane, William G. "Additional Letters of Sydney Smith," *Harvard Library Bulletin*, IX (1955), 397–402.

Lewis, Lady Theresa, ed. *Extracts of the Journals and Correspondence of Miss Berry*. London: Longmans, Green, 1865. III, 358–60, 452,

460–61. Letters which the N. C. Smith edition has only in part are found in III, 469, 472, and 482–83.

Prestige, G. L. *St. Paul's in its Glory: A Candid History of the Cathedral 1831–1911.* London: SPCK, 1955. Pp. 249–56.

Russell, Lord John, ed. *Memoirs, Journal and Correspondence of Thomas Moore,* abridged ed. London: Longman, Green, Longmans, and Roberts, 1860. Pp. 675–76.

5. *Selections*

Auden, W. H., ed. *The Selected Writings of Sydney Smith.* New York: Farrar, Straus and Cudahy, 1956.

Smith, Nowell C., ed. *Selected Letters of Sydney Smith.* London: Oxford University Press, 1956.

II. SELECTED SECONDARY SOURCES

BULLETT, GERALD. *Sydney Smith: A Biography and a Selection.* London: Michael Joseph, 1951. This biography uses some previously unpublished material in discussing Smith's relationship with his father and reproduces otherwise unavailable extracts from Smith's notebooks.

BURDETT, OSBERT. *The Rev. Smith, Sydney.* London: Chapman and Hall, 1934. Burdett concentrates on Smith's philosophy as found in the *Elementary Sketches of Moral Philosophy.*

CHEVRILLON, A. *Sydney Smith et la Renaissance des Idées libérales en Angleterre au XIXe siècle.* Paris: Hachette, 1894. Intended primarily to introduce Smith to a French audience, this book comments briefly on Smith and the Whig-Liberal tradition and summarizes generous selections of Smith's writings.

CLIVE, JOHN L. *Scotch Reviewers:* The Edinburgh Review *1802–1815.* Cambridge: Harvard University Press, 1957. A survey of the early days of the *Review,* this book is a valuable source of literary and political data.

HOLLAND, LADY [SABA]. *A Memoir of the Rev. Sydney Smith.* 2 vols. London: Longman, Brown, Green, and Longmans, 1855; New York: Harper, 1855. This first biography, by Smith's daughter, is still the best. It says little about Smith's writings, but it is a full and intimate portrait of his family and social life. The second volume, a selection of Smith's letters by Mrs. Sarah Austin, is outdated.

HOUGHTON, [RICHARD MONCKTON MILNES], LORD. "The Rev. Sydney Smith," *Monographs: Personal and Social.* London: John Murray, 1873; New York: Holt and Williams, 1873. This is the best of several such personal sketches of Smith.

Selected Bibliography

K[INGSLEY], C[HARLES]. "Sidney Smith," *Fraser's Magazine*, LII (1855), 84–91. A churchman and a political liberal himself, Kingsley appreciates Smith's unique combination of clerical morality and secular wit.

KIRKLAND, WILLIAM. "Character and Opinions of the Late Rev. Sydney Smith," *Godey's Ladies Book*, XXXIII (1846), 35–39. This article is typical of mid-nineteenth century opinion of Smith in American literary circles, appreciative of his political liberalism but suspicious and resentful of his writings on the United States.

MURPHY, JAMES. "Some Plagiarisms of Sydney Smith," *Review of English Studies*, XIV (1938), 199–205. Murphy points out Smith's extensive borrowings in *Elementary Sketches of Moral Philosophy* and *Sermons* (1846). Since both volumes were published posthumously by Smith's widow, apparently contrary to Smith's own intentions, "plagiarism" seems too strong a word.

PEARSON, HESKETH. *The Smith of Smiths*. London: Hamilton, 1934; New York: Harper, 1934. This popular biography emphasizes Smith's political opinions and social life.

REID, STUART J. *A Sketch of the Life and Times of the Rev. Sydney Smith*. New York: Harper, 1885. This appreciative biography attempts to place Smith in the mainstream of political and clerical liberalism. It contains a number of memoirs and testimonials by Smith's contemporaries.

RUSSELL, GEORGE W. E. *Sydney Smith*. London: Macmillan, 1905. One in the English Men of Letters series, this book is noncritical, but it is crammed with useful information about Smith's life and work.

SAINTSBURY, GEORGE. "Sydney Smith," *Living Age*, CLXXVII (1888), 780–90; reprinted from *Macmillan's Magazine*, LVII. This is a criticism of Smith as a philistine from the point of view of the "sweetness and light" school.

SMITH, CATHERINE AMELIA. "Narrative for my grandchildren" and "Recollections of Mr. S. Smith's Life and of His Family." Unpublished mss. in the possession of Mr. David Holland. These early attempts at a biography of Smith by his widow were later used by Lady Saba Holland in her *Memoir*.

SCHNEIDER, DUANE B. "Sydney Smith in America to 1900: Two Check Lists," *Bulletin of the New York Public Library*, LXX (1966), 538–43. Schneider lists both American editions of Smith's writings and American writings about Smith.

[STEPHEN, SIR LESLIE]. "Hours in a Library: The First Edinburgh Reviewers," *Cornhill Magazine*, XXXVIII (1878), 218–34. Stephen comments on the effectiveness of Smith's wit as polemic.

"SYDNEY SMITH as a Minister of Religion," *Biblical Repertory and Princeton Review*, XXVIII (1856), 418–43. This anonymous article in an American Presbyterian journal is a violent and unfair attack on Smith by one who apparently considered Smith a religious and national enemy. It is an extreme example of anti-Smith opinion in the United States.

WILLIAMS, STANLEY T. "The Literary Criticism of Sydney Smith," *Modern Language Notes*, XXXVIII (1923), 416–19. Williams concludes, from the scantiness of Smith's literary essays and the narrowness of his judgments, that Smith was not a literary critic at all.

"Works of the Rev. Sydney Smith," *Christian Observer*, L (1850), 388–400. A fair appraisal of Smith's writings and opinions from an Evangelical magazine which necessarily considered him irreligious.

Index